Best Wishes
from Farmer Chris

a signed edition from

GREAT ✦N✦ORTHERN

Farming, Celebs and Plum Pudding Pigs!

The Making of
FARMER CHRIS

by Chris Jeffery
with Chris Berry

GREAT NORTHERN

Great Northern Books
PO Box 1380, Bradford,
West Yorkshire, BD5 5FB

www.greatnorthernbooks.co.uk

Every effort has been made to
acknowledge correctly and contact
the copyright holders of material in
this book. Great Northern Books Ltd
apologises for any unintentional errors
or omissions, which should be notified
to the publisher.

ISBN: 978-1-912101-38-2

Design by David Burrill

CIP Data
A catalogue for this book is available
from the British Library

DEDICATIONS

Kate

*I love you to bits, Kate. My God you have to put up with
some stuff from me, but you are always there. We have
been through so much together on our journey.
I could not have fulfilled so many dreams and ambitions
without you by my side, your constant love, affection
and unending support.
Love you always, Chris x*

Mum & Dad

*I had the best parents in the world.
I had the kind of love that is so very important for us all.
Dad, I miss you every day
Mum, thank you so much for everything you do
This book would not have been possible without you.
Chris x*

FOREWORD

Stephen Bailey

I had been working as a stand-up comedian for 7 years when I got a phone call that would change my career. I had been doing bits and bobs on TV – an episode here or there – then one day in early 2018, I had a phone call from a production company asking me to host their new show *Celebs on the Farm*. I couldn't have been happier. I am obsessed with celebrity and a guilty pleasure for me is a reality show – so it felt like the dream show.

A few weeks later I received an invitation to a pub lunch in London by the producers. Not very showbiz, I thought.

A pub lunch! Something I'd do on a rare Sunday afternoon off with my dad. I was asked to come over and meet the man who would be judge and jury on *Celebs on the Farm* – the man I now know as FC, some of you might recognise as Farmer Chris and in the farming world he is Channel 5's Chris Jeffery.

I was really nervous going to that lunch. We had a real-life farmer, and a trash-talking camp-as-Christmas comedian coming together to anchor Channel 5's latest offering whilst also herding a bunch of celebs. My nerves were shot.

Upon meeting FC, and a few drinks later, the ice was broken, and I think surprisingly for us both (and luckily for the producers) we really hit it off. As we met once again on the farm, the celebs came in and then we were off.

It's hard to explain what happened during our time filming but everyone really came together and for me it was a pleasant reminder that it doesn't matter how different people are, when you bring good people together, magic happens!

Everyone's story is important. And a bunch of city slickers left at the end of filming (myself included) with a new respect for the country and an even greater respect for those who look after the country for us! I got a new BFF and who knows what the future holds. I hope we get another ten series of *Celebs on the Farm*, but if not, I have a friend for life.

Richard Woolfe

Forget Finding Nemo, this is Finding FC!

Casting Farmer Chris is proof that it's not what you know, it's who you know! I knew exactly the type of farmer I wanted to be our 'judge and jury' for *Celebs on the Farm.*

I wanted someone who was authentic, passionate about farming, who had gravitas and also would make tough decisions and carry them through when we were filming.

The farmer also would need to have a great rapport with our fabulous host Stephen Bailey. So, rather than hold mass auditions – we couldn't anyway, as we didn't have the time or the budget – I put the word out to several TV mates, one of whom was a producer of the brilliant Channel 5 series *The Yorkshire Vet*. I also thought in my heart that our farmer would come from Yorkshire – gruff and prickly on the outside and a heart of gold on the inside all wrapped up with that unmistakeable Yorkshire sense of humour.

My friend Lou said she knew exactly someone to fit the bill and within 24 hours I was FaceTiming Farmer Chris.

The truth is I immediately knew we had found our farmer.

Chris was everything we wanted him to be and so much more. When we brought Stephen and Chris together for the first time for a rehearsal day we had to stop after 20 minutes.

They clicked straight away, making each other laugh and had that instant chemistry that makes many still think to this day that they have known each other for years.

I also loved the way Chris took Stephen under his wing to proudly show him and everyone else about the world of farming – a real telly father and son relationship!

And the rest, as they say, is history. Farmer Chris, or The FC as he is affectionately known by all the cast and crew, is an absolute delight on and off camera. Not only is he totally professional throughout the very long filming schedule, he has become a great friend to me and my family.

He is a total natural, he is charming, funny and kind and through him I know we have shown our viewers in an entertaining way, a real insight into farming and the extraordinary people who dedicate their lives to putting food on our table.

Thank you FC.

CELEBS ON THE FARM

What they say about FC

PAUL MERSON
Winner – Series 2

When I first met Farmer Chris I thought, 'What a miserable man!'

I thought there was no way I can stay on the farm with this man being so cold and, again, miserable, but when I got to know him I couldn't believe what a lovely bloke he is. He has so much time for everyone and is so interested in everyone else.

I went on that farm so scared of animals, but Farmer Chris was so assuring and took my fear away.

Thank you so much Chris. I am pleased to call you a friend and looking back to that first day I would never have thought that in a million years.

The saying with you is so true. Never judge a book by the cover.

ARTEM CHIGVINTSEV

Farmer Chris is the best mentor I have ever experienced.

At first you think he is very tough and intimidating, but once you get to know him he is very loving and has so much respect for animals and life on the farm.

I'm honoured to know him and to have been mentored by him.

CAPRICE

Farmer Chris is the best.

Tough on the outside but a teddy bear, so kind and thoughtful on the inside.

Friends forever Chris!!

KADEENA COX

Farmer Chris, the grumpy and harsh farmer that failed very often to keep a cheeky smile off his face, showing his very warm-hearted true self.

Such a lovely man who was genuinely interested in all of us and our story, taking the time to get to know us individually.

His passion for animals and his craft was lovely to see, so hard-working.

I can't wait to visit your farm and your beautiful cows.

DAVID POTTS

I absolutely loved my time on the farm. I knew Chris was a softie at heart.

CHARLIE EDWARDS

Celebs on the Farm was one of the best experiences of my life and helped me grow as a human being. I made friends for life and when it was time to leave I was upset because it felt like we were a family unit.

Chris was a great boss and it made me realise that life will always go on when my boxing career comes to an end and there are so many other things I could do.

SANDI BOGLE

Celebs on the Farm was completely out of my comfort zone and I was nervous of the unexpected, but after meeting Farmer Chris my experience on the show became one of my most memorable times on TV.

The show provides many challenges but Chris managed to make me laugh during things when I would normally scream.

Such a lovely guy to work with.

LINDA ROBSON

I have just finished Farmer Chris's book and filming *Celebs on the Farm*. It is one of the most interesting reads I've ever had. He's had quite an eventful life. Chris talks about the mental health of farmers, who often lead isolated lives.

KERRY KATONA

I had a fabulous time filming *Celebs on the Farm* and getting to know Farmer Chris. I learned so much about farming and especially about farmers' well-being.

NATALIE WOODS
Celebs on the Farm – Talent Producer

When all of the celebrities arrive from their glamorous lives one of the first people they meet is Farmer Chris. Most of them think he just milks cows, but over the course of filming they understand what he does, day-in, day-out, how hard he works and how much passion and love he has of being a farmer. They become very fond of him.

CHAPTERS

CHAPTER 1

Things really did get better –
as D:ream sang they would

August 2018

I'm in the bright lights of London's West End with a very scantily-clad Charlotte Dawson on one arm and Megan McKenna on the other, with one of TV's hottest new stand-ups just behind me. I'm dressed in the archetypal farmer attire of checked shirt, flat cap, jeans and work boots. I can't really believe what's happening. The 'paps' are shouting instructions for the girls to walk in a certain way, flick their hair, smile, pout.

There's a call to Megan. 'Keep your dress down! They'll try and photograph your knickers as you get in the car.' It is all a bit bedazzling and bewildering for a country boy like me from Yorkshire. This was just like you see on the telly. Then it came to me. I am on the telly. I'm Farmer Chris.

February 1994

I'm at the lowest point in my life. I'm separated from my wife of the past 15 years. I've had an affair. I've just lost my job. I have negative equity in my house, I'm struggling to pay my mortgage and I have no car. I'm in a mess. I blame myself for it all and I'm even receiving counselling from a psychotherapist. I live in the middle of a large village just north of York that has houses, shops, pubs and hundreds of people but I feel so alone.

I go to the garage, get my bicycle out and start pedalling

in the direction of Overton, five miles from where I live in Haxby, to the grass paddock where Dad used to take me and my brothers on a Sunday morning. Dad loved trains and he'd tell us this was the fastest stretch of track in the country as it is perfectly straight. This is ideal.

Almost immediately I'm there a train roars by at 120 miles per hour. This will do. I look at the track, I'm climbing over the fence and walking directly into the middle of it. This is it. Easy. Just wait for the tracks to whistle. I won't feel a thing. Everything I'd ever hoped for is gone. Nothing left.

I look over to the grass paddock and suddenly I see Dad. He is smiling and smoking his pipe. He is wearing his blue woolly jumper and he is waving at me. My brothers are with him, playing and Mum is there with a picnic.

That's when it hits me. I have two wonderful children who need me. I'm their father and I need to be there when they get home from school. I cycle home still feeling very low, but I've found out something more about myself, that I have to carry on for both myself and my children. I get home, put the radio on and D:ream's big hit 'Things Can Only Get Better' is played. It is my inspiration. I'm father Chris.

January 2011

I'm in the Maldives on the 315-yard-long island of Komandoo. I'm down on one knee on the shores of the Indian Ocean and asking Kate 'will you marry me?' It is the most romantic thing I've ever done, in one of the most romantic parts of the world.

Kate says, 'You daft bugger, what are you saying?' and then, 'Of course I will.' It is a magical, lovely moment on our own in one of the most wonderful, amazing places in the world. I'm going to become, for the third time, husband Chris.

April 2015

I'm sat on a sow. That's a female pig to the uninitiated. TV vet Julian Norton, now hugely popular in *The Yorkshire Vet* series is behind the sow with a bottle of semen, all set to artificially inseminate Elsie, my favourite sow. I'm sat there because my role is to act as the boar, preparing the way, so to speak. Now I don't want you getting any wrong ideas and believe me you may get one or two through this book, but I've done this all my life. I'm a pig man. If a sow is on heat and you want it impregnating rather than using an actual boar, you sit on its back.

Julian takes the top off the bottle of semen, spunk to those of a certain volition, and TV history is made. He's the first vet to ever receive what some now call a 'facial' on the television. The girls from the production company are laughing their boobs off.

Today

The pig incident was five years ago and I still have farmers coming into my country store who remember it vividly. Who would have known that through my involvement in *The Yorkshire Vet* it would lead to me being in London's West End three years later with Les Dawson's gorgeous, beautiful daughter on one arm, a stunningly attractive *X Factor Celebrity* winner on the other; and have as my best friend one of the country's leading new showbiz talents Stephen Bailey.

I've certainly gone a long way down the track, and in the most amazing way, rather than going down another type of track looking back on that day in February 1994. I've had two fantastic series of *Celebs on the Farm* on

Channel 5Star and by the time you're reading this I will have completed the third series this time for MTV. I've a great business that Kate and I have grown together and I have my own farm in North Yorkshire with my fabulous rare breed Whitebred Shorthorn cattle and of course my plum pudding pigs.

And if you think those events mentioned so far are a bit up and down then fasten your seat belts for the bumpy ride that is the making of Farmer Chris.

CHAPTER 2

Before I take you back to the beginning, here's a taster of what it is like down on the farm in Celebs on the Farm

The whole TV experience has been and continues to be quite amazing. From the moment Julian (Norton) arrived with the camera crew to film our first *Yorkshire Vet* scene at Spring View Farm in the tiny hamlet that is Thornton on the Hill it has been quite incredible. *Celebs on the Farm* has been an amazing experience and I have loved every minute of my recent showbiz career. Guess I'm a bit of a showman at heart, but I also truly like creating something that others can share and enjoy too.

Filming for *Celebs on the Farm* isn't on my farm. For the first two series it was based at Andrew Dunlop's Lunsford Farm in the village of Pett, just a mile or so off the south coast in East Sussex. It is the most fabulous location and the views are amazing. I stayed at a hotel in Rye, which is about 8 miles away. The Old Borough Arms was ideal for me and my Jack Russell terrier Peggy, who always comes with me and is often seen in the show. Ian and Sarah, who manage the hotel, are most welcoming, as is Lisa Wall, the hotel cook.

Lisa is a Farmer Chris fan. She seems to think I am a star! I find this quite astonishing but since being on the telly I have had so many people who have been so complimentary about me, the show and what I do – farm!

People want a selfie with me and some ask for a signed photo! I even got a pair of knickers sent to me in the post!

But the ultimate, for me, came in June 2019 when I was asked by my good friend Jessie Secker, daughter of family friends Stuart and Barbara Smallwood, to open my old school's village fete in Wigginton near York. It is all really quite surreal, but yes, I love it!

Filming is harder than I thought it would be. It's a totally different environment to what I am used to and the people involved in *Celebs on the Farm* are all TV stars who know about cameras and looking good in front of it. The days are long with 12 hours' filming each day being common. There is a lot of waiting around and even though I feature a lot in the show there is still plenty of downtime while cameras relocate for different shots. There are at least 4 cameras on us at any one time and often 5, plus a drone for outdoor scenes.

Sometimes you're almost through filming a particular sequence and suddenly, from out of what seems nowhere, a plane will fly over leading to the sequence perhaps having to be started all over again.

Stephen (Bailey), the show's presenter, and I ad-lib a lot off each other and he is marvellous at helping me. He's a true professional and we have a great chemistry that I feel comes across really well.

We film 10 episodes in 10 days, but I arrive at the farm a day before we start filming to meet the production team, get my scripts, familiarise myself with the layout of the farm, find out a little about the celebs, many of whom I've never heard of, and the tasks they will have to undertake. I also spend time with Stephen going through scripts and what we're going to do in the show.

The barn we use for each morning's briefing and evening elimination scenes is also where Channel 5 bring their PR teams and organise the series' promotional shots of the celebs, Stephen and I. In the first series it took hours for Charlotte Dawson and Megan McKenna to get

Farming, Celebs and Plum Pudding Pigs!

ready. They'd brought in their own hair stylists and make-up teams, and when I saw them it really was unbelievable. I had never seen anyone look so perfect. It really is a different world this TV malarkey!

Having Peggy with me is great. I love my dog and it's nice to have a little bit of home with me while I'm away. Filming starts about 9am every morning but I have to be on the farm by 8am to get ready, to talk about the day's events to come with the producers, rehearse my lines with Stephen and have coffee. Peggy and I always get up early and in those first two series I would take her to the beach for a long walk on the way to the farm. There is a massive stretch of shingle beach and Peggy loved retrieving her ball from the sea.

It was really special filming the show at Lunsford Farm. It is a lovely traditional family farm and family has always been at the heart of my life, along with one or two other things from time to time!

CHAPTER 3

Born: Saturday 4 January 1958

(10 days overdue)

*Not as Farmer Chris but as farmer's son
Chris Jeffery*

My family mean the world to me. We're not a big family by
any means, but we're close. My parents gave me and my
brothers a wonderful start in life and nothing was ever too
much trouble. They didn't have much money and worked
hard so that we never went without. They are my heroes.
My childhood and my farming background going back
three generations has had a massive influence on the rest
of my life.

I was born 10 days later than my mum's due date in
Fulford Maternity Hospital. If I'd been born on time I
should have made my first appearance on Christmas Day
1957. It is the only time I have ever been late in my life!
I am a stickler for time keeping and cannot abide poor
timekeepers, as some of my *Celebs on the Farm* have
found out!

My mum and dad, Bill and Margery, were living in a
council house in Wigginton at the time, at 4 Saxford Way,
where they had moved into when they married in 1955.
Grandad Bob and my nana Bertha had bought Oak Lea
Farm in Wigginton in 1947. It's still there and is right in
the middle of the village, just two doors away from the
Black Horse pub. The village was much smaller in those
days with a couple of farms and a few houses. Dad worked

for Grandad, but there wasn't enough work for either of them at Oak Lea Farm, as it was only small, so they both also worked for another farmer.

Here's how the Jeffery family came to be in Wigginton. We seem to have been a slightly nomadic family all around the periphery of York up until 1947.

Bob and Bertha had moved from Ferry Farm in Acaster Selby with my dad Bill, my aunt Ellen and my uncle John, who they had adopted when he was just six weeks old back in 1940, which is also the same year they arrived at Ferry Farm from Strensall. My aunt Peggy didn't move to Wigginton with them, she stayed with my nana's sister in Fulford and married a man called Bob Martin who was very highly ranked in the military and they went to live in Germany.

My great-grandad, George Jeffery, had farmed at Town End Farm in Appleton Roebuck. He'd had three sons – my grandad Bob (Robert), Matt (Matthew) and Jonny (Jonathan). Matt was the eldest. They all farmed with George. Jonny then became a butcher and opened a butcher's shop in Fishergate in York.

As far as I can tell what seemed to happen was a little bit of a fall-out, as there often is within farming families when people don't see eye-to-eye with each other over decisions and the farm at Appleton Roebuck was sold, with what I am led to believe the majority of the proceeds going into developing the butcher's shop. Matt, whose wife had died, found another woman called Maude and he cleared off with her and had a lovely life in Adel near Leeds. Word was that they always used to say about her, 'Aye, she's got a bit o' brass 'as this woman.' That just left my grandad Bob with my great-grandad George at Strensall, where they moved to after Appleton Roebuck.

My uncle John, who turned 80 in 2020 and my last remaining Jeffery relative of that generation, tells me that Ferry Farm, which was a mixed farm, as many were back then, was very hard work. They had cattle, sheep, pigs, poultry and arable land. It was an old, cold, damp farmhouse and John says my nana used to go to the fields in springtime, literally on her hands and knees, to thin sugar beet. By doing so she told him in later years that she used to earn enough money to buy shoes for her children.

Grandad Bob never owned Ferry Farm. It was a rich businessman from Leeds who owned land and property and I remember my nana saying she and Grandad were 'hinds', farm 'hinds', which meant they looked after the farm for this man, so they were never even regarded as farm managers. I suppose 'farm hind' was a colloquialism for farmhand and that they were simply seen as this man's employees. They would have been paid a very poor wage to be there. I don't even know whether the animals on the farm ever belonged to Grandad.

The early winter months of 1947 were the coldest and harshest in living memory with snow falling every day from early January to the middle of March. It was known as the 'Big Snow'. The snow would have been bad enough, but when it melted the River Ouse overflowed and flooded out Ferry Farm and many more besides. It also flooded the farmhouse, going in through the windows, and the family had to live upstairs.

It was not long after that, in April, when my grandad and nana bought Oak Lea Farm in Wigginton. How they managed to buy it if they hadn't owned their previous farm at Acaster Selby I don't know, but they didn't take on a large acreage.

Auntie Ellen was 20 at that time and had become a nurse and ended up nursing all over the world, as you'll find out in more detail a little later here. She never married and worked as a nurse for BP (British Petroleum) wherever they had a refinery. They had hospitals at each of them.

Dad was 17 when he came to Wigginton and bless him, he was a very shy man in the matrimonial department, certainly it appears compared to my exploits! How he met my mum was through a blind date in 1949. It was love at first sight.

What happened was Dad had a mate called Fred Bird, who wasn't so shy and told my dad one day to go into town with him into York and meet these women. Fred was a farmer and had a girlfriend called Dorothy who was a nurse training in York. Dad, apparently, was full of trepidation, but off he went with his goggles on and on his trusty Royal Enfield motorbike with half a dozen farming lads on their bikes too. They went into this pub, met these trainee nurses and that's where he met my mum, Margery. The rest, as they say, is history.

But for the record, Mum was staying in the old County Hospital in York that had rooms for nurses. Mum qualified and then became a staff nurse working in all the hospitals in York. She ended her nursing days in The Younger Disabled Unit in York District Hospital.

Mum and Dad married in Hull, where she comes from, and went on honeymoon in London in 1955. Dad said it was his favourite year as York City got to the semi-finals of the FA Cup. He was a big York City fan. They played Newcastle United at Hillsborough and drew 1-1. It went to a replay at Roker Park in Sunderland and they lost 2-0. Dad reckoned York City had been robbed!

Uncle John was only 7 when Grandad and Nana moved to Oak Lea Farm. He wasn't interested in farming. He took a job as driver for a firm of plumbing merchants called Shouksmiths in York and other subsequent jobs. He married auntie Wendy and has been known as Mr Wigginton for years.

Dad worked with my grandad, but there wasn't enough

work to justify both of them, so Dad got a job working on a dairy farm for Robin Midgley at Manor Farm in Wigginton. Robin had a brother, Brian, who was best man at Mum and Dad's wedding. The Midgleys had two farms in Wigginton and Dad worked for both of them, as well as contracting himself out for work on other farms.

Mum stayed in nursing for a long time. She continued to work after each of my brothers and I were born. I was first in 1958, Andrew in 1963, David in 1966 and Ian in 1969. In my early years, from the times I first remember, it seemed Mum was always going 'on holiday to hospital for a rest', not because she was a nurse either. As I got older, I understood why. She was losing babies, bless her. She lost four in all – and all girls. So tragic. She and Dad were trying desperately to get a girl – and she ended up with four boys.

When I think back about mum always being in hospital, because of what she was going through it makes me feel very sad for her and my dad. It must have been so difficult for them emotionally.

At that time, I was being pushed on to Nana at Oak Lea. Obviously I wasn't aware of it happening more than it perhaps should have, if Mum hadn't such bad luck with babies, but I loved it. You have no idea how much I loved my nana. I cry even now thinking about her. And she loved me.

Geographically, No 4 Saxford Way to Nana's was the same as from my farmhouse to the furthest of my two livestock sheds – no more than 60 yards.

I adored Nana. I was this tiny little person and she was this older person hardly ever seen without a pinny on. She loved children. She used to say, 'Don't worry about your grandad and me, we've had our turn.' Nana had this lovely, big old-fashioned range in the kitchen and the kettle was always on. There was the smell of fresh bread constantly being baked.

Being a farm with livestock, I also remember Grandad used to kill a pig once a year, salt it down and it would be put into the back pantry.

They had what was called a 'safe', which was a mesh kind of thing, a cupboard where you put your jug of milk. We're talking the early 60s here, Nana didn't have a fridge. The milk always had a cloth over it with beads all around it to hold it down so the flies couldn't get in.

It was a beautiful farmhouse and was so warm, friendly and happy. It must have been heaven compared to the farmhouse at Ferry Farm! Every Monday, Nana would do the washing with a peggy tub (it's also known as a dolly tub), a peggy stick (also known as a posser or washing dolly stick) and a mangle and wringer. The wash house was just outside.

One lasting memory I have of Oak Lea Farm is when it came to thrashing time – that's an old agricultural expression by the way, for those of you reading this who may be getting the wrong idea! Thrashing time is also known as threshing and is basically what harvesting grain is all about. Lesson over. Future celebs on the farm, I hope you're taking note.

Thrashing time was when all the men would come around, as these were the days when harvest would involve far more than today's combine harvester activity, and Nana would put on this most wonderful display of food in the barn when breaks were taken. I remember so well what she used to call shortcake and how she made it.

This makes me salivate just thinking about it. Once she finished her main baking she would collect up all the pastry she had left, put a bit of sugar on it and add butter and sultanas. She would then fold it up and put it in the oven. When the shortcakes were ready she would take them out and put on hot butter. Oh my (or to some of my

Celebs on the Farm friends, OMG) they were absolutely gorgeous, melt-in-the-mouth treats that I can still taste writing about them here.

I was five years old when my brother Andrew was born and during that time mum had been in and out of hospital. I must have become so used to being with Nana that I would go into the bathroom in our house that looked out over to Nana's and shout 'Nana, come and get me, they're being cruel!' which of course Mum and Dad never were, they were brilliant parents, but I was a kid and like most grandparents my nana thought the world of me.

Nana would come round and say, 'What are you doing to that child?' I'm sure she meant it affectionately as there wasn't a bad bone in her body, but thinking about it as I write this now I bet this really upset Mum. She was a young mother losing children, stillborn, fully formed. Imagine the trauma she was going through. Nowadays she would have support workers left, right and centre.

There was none of that and Mum was still working all the hours God sent. And there was me, this little brat shouting to my nana, 'Come and get me, they're being cruel'. Mum, all I can say is I love you very much and you have given me everything, you and Dad.

And it wasn't that Mum was never there. Ours was a three-bedroom, semi-detached house with no heating apart from the fire. I would watch *Watch with Mother* in black and white, not colour, with my mum. *Andy Pandy* was my favourite and *The Woodentops*. After that the test card would come on until teatime. My bedroom was a tiny box room with only enough space for a bed and a bedside cabinet. I remember being scared of the dark and so Mum bought me this Humpty Dumpty night light that she would plug in when I went to bed. So much for big, stern Farmer Chris!

Sunday mornings. Wow! The radio was always on with

programmes like *Family Favourites* and *Housewives' Choice* as mum cooked our Sunday roast. We always ate together. There was no telly on and this was of course way before mobile phones.

We had beef one week and pork the next. I can still smell the Yorkshire puddings and roast potatoes cooking. There were always lots of Yorkshire puddings and we had them with our Sunday roast with gravy, and also with golden syrup as pudding. Dad would always have a shandy with his meal, and me and my brothers would be treated to a glass of lemonade – it was water for us during the rest of the week.

Mum always made sure there was enough meat left from the roast joint she had cooked, so that there was sufficient for Monday night's tea. All of our vegetables were home-grown as Dad had the back garden full of them, as well as having an allotment. I honestly don't know where he made the time for working on farms, contracting, gardening and looking after us; and Mum too, with her nursing and all the times she'd had in hospital, getting myself and my brothers' washing done, making meals, tidying and cleaning, fetching and carrying. They were both fabulous parents in every way.

Dad loved listening to popular singers from that time, just before Cliff Richard and The Beatles became famous, like Jim Reeves, Frank Ifield, Slim Whitman, Nat King Cole, Bing Crosby and Val Doonican. All that kind of slow, soft, gentle sound, almost country music.

He could also play the mouth organ (harmonica) and when we were having a bath, me and my brothers, he'd play it to us while he was sat on the loo, with the lid down! The only tune he really knew was 'I'll Take You Home Again, Kathleen'.

We all had to have a bath every night and like many families we all shared the water, one in, one out. It was us four boys first, then Mum, then Dad. We had a small coalhouse, as our only heating was the coal fire. I remember getting up early with Dad in the winter to help him as he lit the fire before going to work, to warm the house before Mum got up.

Mum loved classical music. I love music and always have, but all high-pitched noises and music from some ballet or other, it drove me mad! Mario Lanza, symphony orchestras and opera – oh my God, opera – turn it off mum! Mum is now André Rieu's biggest fan and has travelled all over to see him.

We had a radiogram, one of those that was in a wooden cabinet on legs with an inbuilt record player turntable and radio. It was in the dining table end of the room. I remember the radio had to 'warm up' before it would work. Our house was always full of music. I remember standing in my room singing along into a hairbrush, as a microphone, to 'Do Wah Diddy Diddy' by Manfred Mann; The Beatles' 'Hey Jude' and 'Nights in White Satin' by The Moody Blues.

We had a couple of pets, my budgie Joey and a tortoise called Fred, who I thought was brilliant. I would feed him lettuce leaves from Dad's vegetable garden in summer. He used to walk around the garden. I remember being devastated when I took him out of his hibernation box one springtime and he had died.

I had fantastic Christmases at home with Mum, Dad and all the family around. There'd be uncle John and auntie Wendy and their children, my cousins; Nana and Grandad and auntie Ethel, my nana's sister who used to come and stay with her. How we ever got everybody in I don't know, but wow, was it great!

Nana would come and see us Christmas morning with a proper old stocking that included a bit of coal wrapped in silver foil. The food was amazing and I don't know how we ate it all. I can't eat that much now! They were lovely times. We would watch telly, play with presents and just have fun. There was never any fall outs, after all it was Christmas!

I'd always wanted to be a farmer from what must have been around 4 years old. I had toy tractors, as well as proper metal Matchbox cars and Corgi cars, and I had all the farming gear and my own pair of wellies. Farming was my life, as well as playing like any other kid.

My favourite present was my train set. I went from a quite small set in my bedroom to this 8ft x 4ft plywood board that Dad got hold of to make a proper track layout. It was such a difficult thing in those days to get the electric to it. I had a transformer that you turned around to make it go faster. Dad loved it too. Oh, how he loved train sets. We had this one engine where you put drops into the funnel and as it went along it would puff out the smoke like a real steam engine.

Dad loved real trains even more. We didn't live so far away from the York to Edinburgh line and often on a Sunday morning he'd say 'let's have a cup of coffee and go and watch the trains' and we would all get into the car and go to Overton, which took about ten minutes. In those days there was nothing to stop you parking on the bridges and walking down on to the line. This bit of track from Darlington to York is practically straight so you can see for miles. I used to love going and watching the Deltics that all had names like Royal Highland Fusilier.

Our Sunday mornings were spent watching trains at various bridges along the line. After trains had passed at Overton we would drive through the village and stop at the next one and go round to Beningbrough a bit further north. We'd take in something like four to six bridges each week. They went past at was a very scary speed and we were really close to them.

Grandad was a staunch Methodist, as was his father, my great-grandad George who had been a local lay preacher. Grandad always dressed well, whether for church or when he was ploughing the fields. He'd wear a jacket, shirt and tie, a pair of corduroy trousers and boots – and he would always be whistling hymns.

Mum and Dad didn't follow in his chapel footsteps, but they always watched *Songs of Praise* on telly. They sent me to Sunday School at Haxby Methodist Chapel and I hated going with a passion because I wanted to be doing something more interesting with Dad or Grandad on the farm. They didn't make me go for long. I think they quickly realized it wasn't for me.

The most wonderful thing I remember as a child growing up on the farm were my grandad's horses, Tommy and Laddy. I guess he must have brought them from Ferry Farm. Grandad farmed with Shire horses and was probably one of the last, certainly in our area, to work the land with them. I would spend a lot of time watching him getting them ready for work and, as I grew up, helping him.

Tommy was a chestnut and the old stager; Laddy was a big, black, strong, young horse and Grandad worked him alongside Tommy to train him. When I was a little older I would help Grandad on the farm. He had cattle and pigs. There was a fold yard, pig buildings, a barn with hay and straw and a turnip shed. He used to grow turnips for winter fodder. The majority of the farm was down to arable land.

When I'd come home from school I would go and fetch Tommy back home. He'd be a very old horse by this time, in his mid-20s, and I'd collect his halter from the barn, go down Church Lane, climb on the gate so that I could get his halter on. Tommy would always know to come to the gate. I'd then jump on his back and ride him home bareback through the village to Grandad's farm. It was a journey of what was probably no more than about 300-400 yards but I'd look forward to it every night.

I'd be with Grandad quite a lot with his horses and he would let me drive the horse and cart when he was with me. It would be a flat cart and we would be picking up hay or we would be picking up turnips. I never drove or rode Laddy though. He was too strong for me.

One of my saddest memories as a child was when Tommy had to be put down. My grandad was a lovely man and I know how much Tommy meant to him. He had bought him as a 5-year-old and retired him at 25. One day I noticed Tommy wasn't walking very well and I told Grandad. I could tell by Grandad's face that this wasn't good. The next day, after school, I went to the field where Tommy would normally be, and he wasn't there. I found Grandad and I could see he was upset, but he somehow controlled his emotions because he was more worried about mine.

Grandad sat me down and told me Tommy had gone to sleep and wouldn't wake up. I found out later in life that Grandad had called the vet and had Tommy put down in the field. Grandad had stayed with him while the vet did the job. For Grandad the loss of Tommy was like losing a member of the family. I remember crying that night.

These were the days of the 60s when men in fields were stooking the sheaves. All the stooks would then be brought back into the farmyard in the Dutch barn where they would be stored until the threshing machine came around. Those old farming scenes of all that work going on were incredible, but that was the way in which the grain was dried and processed in those days.

Playing outside was the done thing in the 60s. There were no computer games or electronic devices of any kind, no mobile phones. We played, and my did we play. We were quite lucky where we lived as all around us were fields and ponds. We just went into the fields, played hide-and-seek, tied ropes to branches in trees, swung across ponds and occasionally dropped off into them. It was probably quite dangerous and now that kind of thing is completely something you wouldn't let your kids go off and do, but we had fun all the same and fortunately nobody of our groups ever suffered badly. We were just having fun.

We would make our own go-karts. I had a friend called Phil Duston, the son of a local joiner and in those days joiners were invariably also the local coffin makers. I'd go into his dad's workshop and see all these coffins. It was quite scary.

Phil was a dab hand at making a go-kart out of scraps of his dad's wood and wheels off prams. I have no idea where he got these wheels from, but they never seemed to be in short supply!

We'd make go-karts, which was a wonderful, fulfilling thing to do, and we'd then have this competition to see whose go-kart could last the longest as we rammed into each other.

There was a very small hill going down from the end of Saxford Way past the village shop and across the main road. Whoever drew the short straw would be coming up the hill, which meant whoever was coming down it had the best chance of winning. We used to ram each other like mad with these bloody go-karts with one man (boy) steering and another pushing. Crazy mad, but we were making our own entertainment – and often we were back to Phil's workshop for much needed repairs.

Saxford Way was also a cricket ground on a night-time in summer. It was a no-through road. Dad would set up the stumps. He was into his cricket and played for the village team along with all the local farming lads. I have a silver cup he won for most runs scored.

All the kids would come out to play at 'The Saxford Way Oval', which was just our street. There would be Barry Gill, Janet Robinson, Rob Driffield and even Mr Doughty who lived next door would come and turn his arm over with the odd googly every now and then. It was a great way to spend a summer's night and like any time of year you'd only come in when it was dark.

Dad was such a wonderful father. He'd come home after spending long hard hours on farms and always had the energy and time to play with me. We'd play-fight and play cricket, as well as other games. He loved watching his football.

We would always go to Scarborough for a week's holiday in summer. Dad would get us all in the kitchen to get our shoes cleaned. The car, we had a great big old black automatic Wolseley, was brought round on the Friday night and we all had to be up for 7 o'clock on Saturday morning to set off. We always had to get up early one morning on holiday, about 6 o'clock, so that we could watch the fish being landed at the harbour.

We never appeared to have much money but Dad managed to run the Wolseley. I think he maybe only taxed it for 6 months of the year as we only seemed to use it from April to October. We'd rent our own flat and get a chalet on Scarborough's South Bay near The Spa. We spent every day on the beach and our chalet housed a kettle, a stove, our deckchairs and acted as our own little store. At the end of each day we were allowed half an hour in Jimmy Corrigan's amusement arcade next to The Futurist Theatre where we tried our luck with bags of pennies and ha'pennies.

Before that, of course, we had to play cricket on the beach and the thing with Dad was he would always get everybody else involved. We'd go on donkey rides and Jumping Jimmy's, the old trampolines. They were all part of the week. Dad wasn't much for the amusement park with the big wheel near the harbour, but we used to go fishing with nets in the rock pools. Ours was your archetypal, old-fashioned 60s family holiday, which I looked forward to every year.

As I got a bit older we stayed in a hotel in Scarborough one time, The Dorchester. I remember them ringing the bell for dinner one night. The height of posh for us!

We would also go to Hull Fair every year. It's one of the biggest travelling fairs in Europe. We spent a lot of time going over there as my mum is from Hull, but I really didn't like going. We would go over to see Gran who lived in a terraced house with uncle Peter and uncle Laurie. I'm a country boy. I didn't want to go to this city. I was bored out of my mind when we went, so Dad would take me to the park so I could play on the swings, but I enjoyed going to Hull Fair. It was all candy floss, bright lights and noise, a fantastic, unbelievable place.

Back home my favourite comic was *The Victor* and my favourite story was about Alf Tupper, an athlete who was known as The Tough of the Track; my favourite sweets, from Len Hayton's village shop, were things like candy shrimps in a paper bag or pineapple chunks and pear drops. Len's shop had everything, and in those days when you returned empty bottles of pop, you'd get money for returning them. We used to go and gather up as many as we could and buy sweets with the proceeds.

My first school was Wigginton School. It's still there. I didn't really like it. Our village wasn't big at all, certainly not the size it has grown to today, and there were just two classrooms. My first teacher was Miss Brown. Going up to what they called 'big school' was about moving to another school for many kids, but not for us. Ours was the other classroom.

This was the time of free bottled milk arriving in the

morning. The school was heated by this big Aga, which was fired with coke and we all had to take it in turns to fill it so that we kept warm in winter. I made good friends, but my biggest accomplishment was passing my 11-plus examination, and boy did that set me on my way to a great school!

But before we go on let me tell you about a remarkable journey I had when I was just 7 years old.

CHAPTER 4

Africa

Aunt Ellen was a real globetrotter with her work as a nurse for BP. She had a passion for travel and worked in Bermuda, Australia, New Zealand and Hong Kong. She wrote a letter to me in 1965. I didn't really know her, because she had lived away all of my young life, only coming back occasionally at Christmas, but she wrote that she had a lovely villa in Libya in Africa and would I like to have a holiday with her?

This was four years before Gaddafi came on the political scene in the country. Very different times. There wasn't the political tension, but who wouldn't have their doubts about their young son going off on his own, thousands of miles away!

Mum and Dad looked at this letter and I'm sure they thought it was a bit daft, inviting a 7-year-old to travel out there on his own. I just said I wanted to go. It was an adventure and I was up for it. And go I did, in the school summer holidays that year.

Aunt Ellen had planned this very methodically. She'd written to me just after Christmas with the invitation to Benghazi. She organised and paid for everything, but one thing she couldn't sort out was that I needed a passport. Mum and Dad organized it. You had to go to London to get a visa in those days.

All the tickets came through and Mum and Dad took me to the airport. We took the train to King's Cross station and then a taxi to Heathrow. Mum had dressed me in this lovely blazer which included the white rose of Yorkshire.

In those days it was almost like you had to dress up to fly. I was very smart with new short trousers and nice well-polished shoes. All my luggage looked good too.

I remember becoming very scared, yet at the same time very excited when we reached the airport. I'd never been near an aeroplane, let alone go on one. We met the air hostess. The airline knew I would be travelling on my own. Even in 1965 they wouldn't just allow a 7-year-old on a plane without some kind of supervision and so this lady was responsible for me.

What I do remember clearly is there was no security at the airport at all, absolutely none. When you consider what airport security is like today anything could have happened! Mum and Dad saw me off at the last point they realistically could, before letting me go.

The plane was a jet Comet, the first commercial jet, and it was a BOAC flight from Heathrow to Rome. I had mixed emotions. I sat at the window and could see the terminal. I had tears rolling down my face, crying my eyes out as it was now real and the plane was already going so fast, but I soon enjoyed it. A tray of food arrived and it wasn't all plastic like you get now, it was like silver service with napkins and proper knives and forks. I had a glass of orange juice.

Once we touched down in Rome I had to get off that plane and board another to Tripoli. From there I flew to Benghazi with no change of plane. Easy really. For a 7-year-old. Just 2500 miles. Nothing could possibly go wrong could it?

The worst thing ever happened, or at least the worst thing for the stewardess. I got lost. It was in the airport in Rome. The lady must have helped me get off the plane, but maybe she had to go to the loo or to take a break, all I know is that for whatever reason I'd gone wandering off. I was a child enjoying myself and was probably in the sweet shop. I wasn't lost so far as I was concerned, just wandering around in somewhere new. The flight to Tripoli was held up until I was found.

When we touched down in Benghazi I was frogmarched by the stewardess into the terminal. There was absolutely no way she was going to let me out of her sight again. Aunt Ellen was there to meet me. I'd seen her at Christmas sometimes, but that was all. She gave me such a fantastic time. It was unbelievable.

Like most, when it's your first time in a hot country, I found it just that, so hot. My first thought was that I didn't know how I would survive in the heat of summertime in North Africa.

Aunt Ellen had an old Volkswagen Beetle. It was a blue turquoise colour and had beaded seats. She had a manservant at her villa. Different world to Wigginton!

Benghazi is on the coast and Aunt Ellen taught me to swim in the Mediterranean Sea. She was a good swimmer. I always seem to have had problems with my feet, which we will come to more later, and remember cutting a toe on a stone when learning to swim. The sand was so hot I couldn't stand on it for long. Maybe that's why I learned to swim!

We went to the market in Benghazi every day, to buy fresh fruit. That's when I saw these massive watermelons and other food I'd never tasted before. It was while I was with Aunt Ellen that I first had spaghetti Bolognese, hardly a Libyan dish I know, but I'd never had it before. I can still taste it, thinking about it now, with Parmesan cheese.

There were a lot of 'firsts' for me while with Aunt Ellen. It was the first time I had seen beggars on the street, people with just one leg, blind people, it was a culture shock even for a 7-year-old – with only one street in Wigginton at the time you didn't see many people let alone beggars!; I rode a camel in the Sahara Desert; I slept in a hammock on the balcony, with a mosquito net around me, just for one night – as I'd begged Aunt Ellen to let me sleep outside. I had a fan in my room, but there was no air conditioning like there is today; and I met my first girlfriend! She was called Lesley and she was younger than me, she was blonde-haired, and I must have met her while on the beach. We played together on the sand. Hardly romance. There's enough of that to come!

I had the most wonderful time with Aunt Ellen. She showed me so much, introduced me to so many new things and with the weather being so hot I came back as brown as a berry.

I flew back direct from Benghazi to Heathrow. Even the airlines were taking no more chances with me wandering off again! I was a little bit cheeky at the time, a young lad full of mischievousness, a bit cocky with it.

Dad met me at Heathrow and we caught a taxi from there to King's Cross station where I think we missed the train we'd hoped to catch, even though I can remember us running for it with my cases. We took the 'mail train' instead and arrived back into York station about midnight. I was exhausted but exhilarated and with fantastic memories.

The headteacher at Wigginton School was called Mrs Wray. She was a very strict, bossy lady and she hated me. Maybe she was just jealous of my holiday in Libya, but she seemed to hate that I'd been to Africa. I wrote an essay about my whole summer experience of going to Libya and being with Aunt Ellen. I had to stand at the front of the classroom and speak to the class about it

I can remember Mrs Wray saying 'how ridiculous' that a child should go there at my age. She never liked me from then on, until I left the school. I even remember Mum going in to school, or saying that she would, because I would come home crying after Mrs Wray had been awful to me.

CHAPTER 5

From Wigginton to Nunthorpe via my 11-plus qualification

I've really never been that bright, academically. I've had to work hard to get any qualifications and when mum realized I wanted to go down the farming route she was determined that I had back-up, some formal qualifications and she encouraged me to study.

Two of us passed our 11-plus, which is what you had to do in order to get a chance of getting into a grammar school, Brian Hornshaw and Chris Jeffery – me! Mum was elated. But there was only one place up for grabs at the prestigious Nunthorpe Grammar School in York, one of just two all-boys grammar schools in the city. I went for an interview and got in. This changed my life as all of my pals I'd known at Wigginton went to Joseph Rowntree Secondary Modern School in New Earswick.

I remember Mum buying all the stuff. She had a list from the school that included a blue blazer, grey slacks, white shirt and a blue tie with red and white flashes across it, and of course the school cap. Gym gear was all pure white, including plimsolls – and as my 'house' team was Saxon whose colours were yellow I had to have a yellow rugby shirt, white socks, rugby boots and football boots. The other houses were Norman, Celt and Dane.

I've always been the type of person who likes to do well, even if I didn't think I was that bright academically, and I was very proud of being able to have made it to grammar school – even though I did feel a bit of a twat wearing a cap and blazer. I knew my pals in the village would take the mickey of my school appearance but looking back I'm extremely proud to have been there. It's now called Millthorpe and is no longer a single-sex school, but back then we were next door to the Mill Mount Grammar School for Girls.

To get to Nunthorpe from Wigginton I had to catch the bus at around 8 in the morning from the village to Blossom Street in York. It was about six and a half miles. I'd then walk about a mile from there along all the back roads and across Scarcroft Green before reaching the school, which is right at the back of the Knavesmire where horse racing takes place.

It was quite an imposing school with a long driveway going up a hill and lined with poplar trees on either side. It had quite a history and some much more celebrated pupils like Vincent Cable, the former leader of the Lib Dems – a little bit before my time; former England football manager Steve McClaren, who was there around the same time but is a bit younger than me; and actor Mark Addy who has recently appeared in the TV series *White House Farm* and started just after I'd finished. I became good friends with Mick Hagen who went on to star for York Rugby League Football Club – for a big hard lad, boy could he run. He was a fantastic player. I also had another really good mate Nick Thompson.

Sport played a big part of my life at Millthorpe. I represented the school at rugby, cricket, football and volleyball – in my early teens I was turning into a big strapping lad.

We were trained by Peter Bibby who played volleyball for England. At the time I thought it wasn't exactly a macho game, but we were great. We had a fantastic team that travelled all over Yorkshire and we won a few trophies.

Peter was known as 'Big Balls Bibby'. I'm not kidding you, this man had massive balls – and I'm not talking about the ones we used to play with. Poor Peter, having a nickname like that, but I guess some would be proud of it, so maybe he was.

Rugby was my real passion at school. I was a proper No 8 and captained the school team. I had trials for North Yorkshire. That was rugby union but we must have played rugby league at some stage too because I remember playing for school at York RLFC's Clarence Street ground.

I enjoyed playing cricket. I think I got that from Dad and all those sessions back home and on the beach at Scarborough. I was a good fast bowler, right arm over. I played as a goalkeeper in the football team. I quite liked being a goalie. Our arch rivals in all sporting competitions were Archbishop Holgate Grammar School at Badger Hill near the University of York. That was always a crunch game and we hated them just as much as they hated us. It was fantastic rivalry.

One of the greatest times I had at school was our school trip to Austria when I was 14. Once again, where Mum and Dad got the money from I don't know because it wasn't cheap, but we went to Igls near Innsbruck. We took the train from York to London and then to Dover where we crossed to Calais and then took a sleeper train with couchettes, seats that could be changed to sleeping berths. I will never ever forget getting to Innsbruck. People talk about breathtaking scenery. I'd never seen anything like it in my life.

We had 10 nights there and it was brilliant. It is still the only time in my life that I have ever skied and we were on the slopes every day. We saw one girl struggling so much that we nicknamed her Spider, because she was all arms and legs, all over the place. She was a lovely girl, tall with long legs and long blonde hair, but she couldn't ski.

I found I was pretty good at the Apres Ski bit! We drank schnapps and on the bar they had these multi-coloured, hard-boiled eggs as a snack. Maybe the schnapps gave us some Dutch courage because we ended up making our way from our dormitory to where the girls slept.

This was our *Fawlty Towers* moment. Do you remember the one where there's a bedroom scene and Basil (Fawlty) hides in a wardrobe, but is holding the door shut with his finger showing? That was us. Me and my mate Paul Baker.

In fairness we weren't doing anything wrong, apart from being there I suppose, and then we heard someone coming down the corridor. The girls' teachers came into the room because they heard voices and they saw this lone finger holding the door shut.

Paul and I only had our shorts on and so we were half-naked. That made things look even worse when we bolted for it. We shot out of the wardrobe, out of the room and ran straight back to ours. After that we weren't allowed out on the remaining evenings and apparently our little escapade didn't go down too well with our school.

I was beside myself that they were going to tell my mum and dad when we got back but they didn't.

There are always bullies in all walks of life and our school was no different. We had one lad who was a real bastard, a thoroughly horrible lad who bullied everybody. I won't give him the honour of reading his name here, if he's still alive, but he was a nasty piece of work, always upsetting people. While I enjoyed sport, I hate conflict, but one day I saw red.

This particular day we were in a classroom on a lunch break. There were no teachers around. This lad, let's call him Richard Head, was firing a catapult hurting people. I remember bending over to pick something up and ****ing hell did I suddenly get this pain up my arse!

I turned around and saw him laughing at me. That was it. This was the time. I didn't know I had the strength in me like this but I went straight over to him, grabbed him by the scruff of his neck, clenched my fist and I ****ing hit him – bang – right on his nose.

He went down, cracking his head on the side of a desk as he fell. There was blood everywhere. I just stood there watching blood coming out of his nose and his head. Everybody around couldn't believe what I'd done and neither could I.

I didn't know what would happen to me or what would happen to this bully. Would I get the cane from the headmaster, as in those days that's what happened for things like fighting. Would I get expelled? Would this bully die? What would my mum and dad think?

What followed was amazing. I think initially I might have been sent home early that particular day, but the next day when I was called into the headmaster's office fearing the worst, everything went my way. I was sat with my head of Saxon house, Mr King, when the headmaster said, 'We don't really want to say 'well done', but well done Jeffery. We're not condoning what you've done but thank God somebody has stood up to this lad.'

It turned out that the teachers and headmaster didn't know how to deal with him, so I'd done everyone a favour – and I never got the cane.

When the lad that had been the school bully came back he walked up to me, shook my hand and told me he was sorry. He never bullied anyone again, at least not while we were at school together.

It is the only fight I've ever had. All over in one hit. I'm not looking for another, as I wasn't even then. He was a massive lad and if we'd had an actual fight he'd have beaten me. I just happened to be in the right place, or wrong place at the right or wrong time. Whenever I saw him afterwards he'd tell me he still bore the scar from where he'd hit the desk on the way down.

I left school with four 'O' levels in Maths, English, Geography and Art; and CSE grade 2 in French, when I was 16 in 1974. I never got into an A grade for anything, I was always in B, and was never clever enough to study Latin. My school reports always included 'could do better' but when it got to sport it was always 'brilliant, he excels'.

Art was the subject I loved most. I could draw all sorts of things and myself and Mick and Nick – Hagen and Thompson – called ourselves The Gibbons. The comedy TV show and group *The Goodies* were around at the time and we enjoyed being daft and drawing silly things. Our art teacher Brian Khestaven encouraged our messing about in art class, but we had a serious side too and created some nice stuff. We all had our own ways of doing things, our own genre. I used to draw trees and countryside scenes such as farm scenes mainly in pencil. We used to say 'ah good, it's Gibbons-time' when it was art period.

CHAPTER 6

From Saxford Way to Oak Lea Farm

Cockney Rebel, Shelley, Scarborough and my first job on a farm

No 4 Saxford Way was my family home until I was 14 years old when we moved, not very far at all, into Nana and Grandad's house at Oak Lea Farm in 1972. Grandad had been easing down. They decided to move into a pensioner's bungalow in the village. They hadn't had much land at Oak Lea and had decided to sell some of what they had, for building land. Mum and Dad bought the house. The farm itself wasn't big enough to be making a living from on its own, as Dad and Grandad had already realised, so Dad continued working for others.

Mum and Dad only had Oak Lea Farm for around three years before moving again, but these were now my teenage years and boy-oh-boy did I have a good time as I began going to youth club, being with my first proper girlfriend, got together with the guys who were to become my best mates, drank my first pint in a pub, had my first time in bed with a girl, went to agricultural college, went on holiday with the boys, changed our names (we made up new ones for ourselves) and met the girl who I truly fell head over heels in love with and who eventually became my first Mrs Jeffery!

My first pint of beer was Sam Smith's Nut Brown Ale. It was served out of the bottle and cost 14 pence in The Tiger Inn in Haxby. I shall never forget it. It was bloody awful! I couldn't believe what I was doing and my mum and dad would have been mortified as I was drinking ale in a pub at only 15 years old, but Fred, the landlord, like many in those days, turned a blind eye.

I'd gone in to the pub with my next-door neighbour Rob Driffield who lived with his mum, as his dad had died in an accident at work. Rob was a bit older than me, maybe by about 2-3 years and it was he who had mentioned about going to the youth club in Haxby. We would go on a Monday and Wednesday night and that's how the 'going to the pub' started as we would call in at The Tiger at 6.30pm on our way to the club.

Youth club was great for getting to know people! There was this particular young lady called Shelley who went to Queen Anne Grammar School for girls in Clifton in York. Shelley had come with a friend who lived in Haxby. She was a lovely, beautiful girl with long blonde hair and I loved her with all my heart.

I used to love watching her play table tennis as she was very good, but also mainly because she was a very attractive young lady and a nice mover. We got talking and started going out together.

Shelley was the first girl I'd ever touched in any way romantically or lustfully. It was one of those times when I practised kissing my own hand beforehand because I was that concerned about getting it right. How am I kissing? Am I kissing right? What will she think? These were all my concerns as they probably are for many others – and no! *Celebs on the Farm* fans, I did not go around kissing any Shire horses, cattle or pigs! Not that I'm admitting to anyway.

It was all just a bit of heavy petting at the start – but you know where that leads? But listen, I loved her. I fell in love with Shelley. She lived in Gillygate in York. Her dad was a newsagent.

The 70s is still my favourite era of pop music and

I'd be listening to Radio 1 when Tony Blackburn, Noel Edmonds and Dave Lee Travis were all on. I had a small transistor radio, run on batteries, and remember going to bed listening to Radio Luxembourg under the bedsheets so Mum and Dad wouldn't hear it. I also had this big bloody cassette tape thing. I'd take it on the bus with me when I went round to see Shelley at her house. We'd go into her bedroom and play the music – and that's not a euphemism!

Shelley was into this group that hadn't made it big at the time – Steve Harley & Cockney Rebel – and told me the band was coming to York University. We went along and heard all the songs we had been listening to for the last few months. It was a wonderful feeling being there. My first ever gig. It was amazing. My first album was their first, *The Human Menagerie*. I still love Steve Harley's music and would love to meet him one day.

While I shall never forget that gig, maybe 'Come Up & See Me, Make Me Smile', their No.1 hit, fits better for this next unforgettable moment with Shelley.

Shelley had come to see me at Oak Lea Farm. Mum and Dad had gone away on holiday with my brothers, to see Aunt Ellen who had now retired from nursing and had returned to England. She had moved to Ilfracombe in Devon. Shelley came round. We went to bed. We didn't have sexual intercourse. I sound like Bill Clinton denying what happened in the White House here, don't I? But, we honestly didn't. It was just wonderful. I was in bed with this beautiful girl. We were naked together. Unbelievable. I shall never forget that moment. Tender and warm and so special.

'Hot Love' by T Rex was my favourite song of that time and David Bowie was fantastic. I had all of his albums. 'Rebel Rebel' was Shelley's song. She was a bit of a rebel herself and it always reminds me of her. Sweet's

'Blockbuster' and Queen's 'Seven Seas of Rhye' were favourites too.

That same summer I went on holiday with three mates – Mark Benson and Nigel Raven from Nunthorpe Grammar; and Chris Brown from Wigginton, who has his own nurseries business these days. We decided to go to Scarborough for a week and rented a little apartment. Shelley had arranged to come from York in the middle of the week. It all sounded good.

It pissed it down all week and all we lads did was smoke cigarettes, I smoked Embassy Regal; we drank beer and went to the bookies. To cap it all when Shelley arrived I could tell something wasn't right. We went to bed, but she told me she was really sorry, but she'd found somebody else. You've no idea. I was devastated. She said he was also called Chris and was in the Army.

I cannot tell you, even in these words, how mortified I was. I felt sick and I cried my eyes out in front of her. I wanted to go home and tell my mum to please tell her to come back. I absolutely loved this wonderful, happy, cheerful, sexy young girl so much, but that was it. Shelley had gone. I was utterly heartbroken. So much for a nice week away!

I'd say 1974 was still my favourite year for music. Artists like Elton John, Rod Stewart, The Rolling Stones, Queen, Abba, The Bee Gees, David Bowie and Mud were all fabulous and Mud were the resident band at the Cat's Whiskers nightclub in York where the Fab 4 – me, Stuart Smallwood, Rob Dent and Lyle Cass all frequented. I just loved 'Tiger Feet' by Mud.

Stuart, Rob and Lyle, who I'd known all my life, were now with me, the Fab 4 for drinking and going out on the pull.

Stuart's dad was a butcher, Lyle's dad was a farm worker and Rob's dad had a farm on Sutton Road just outside Wigginton. Rob and I were the ones who always liked the girls. I was a bit younger than the other three at 16, they were all 17 or 18.

Rob Driffield was still on the scene but not one of our four, although I got into rugby league with him, going to watch York RLFC. We used to lark about together in the fields where we put up some goalposts and struck goals through them and passed the ball between each other up and down the field. Tragically Rob, who was a joiner, passed away due to asbestosis at just 40.

Back in those days in the mid-70s there always seemed to be a barbecue to go to on a Friday or Saturday night or a village dance. One minute we'd be at the youth club in Wigginton, next we'd be at a dance at Huby, a club in York or at a young farmers' evening at Castle Howard or over in Malton. I remember going in to York to buy a sparkly jacket for an end-of-year dance.

Stuart loved his Ford Corsair 2-litre V8 that had an 8-track cartridge. If you don't know, an 8-track cartridge was 'the thing' to have in the 70s if you were into music. We had T Rex banging away with the windows down as we moved at 80mph.

You'd go to a disco or a gig, you'd expect to get pissed and there was always fighting.

My next girlfriend was Pamela. For whatever reason she got the hots for me, which was pretty amazing because she was an untouchable, she'd been going out with this guy called Ray, but she had finished with him. She was a beautiful brunette who was a bit older than me.

We went to the pictures and the film turned out to be my first X-rated film – *A Clockwork Orange* – at the Odeon in York. For those that don't know it was a very weird film featuring people being beaten up dressed in boiler suits and bowler hats.

All Pamela was interested in was getting her hand

in my trousers! And she did. She stayed with me about a week and then went back to her boyfriend. That's how long it lasted, so I had a week of fun with this beautiful girl from Haxby and off she went. She's still married to him today! My best wishes to you both!

The Cat's Whiskers in York was great. You had to wear a jacket, tie and collar to get in. If we had forgotten our ties, because we were on a night on the town we'd take a sock off, tie it around our necks and get in. Ever resourceful.

I'm not a hoarder but I wish so much I'd kept those albums, all on vinyl, that I had in those days by Bowie and Cockney Rebel.

Me and Rob were the two who were always looking out for the girls. Rob was much more forward than me everywhere we went, and nothing would faze him. He could pull the girls, no matter what. This was the time when lots of blokes drank lager and lime! I liked a pint of lager and still do. By God could we drink too! We'd drink before youth club on a Monday and Wednesday, then we would be on the pull at a barbecue on a Friday, in a night club on a Saturday and at a local pub on a Sunday.

Back in the 70s, agricultural colleges like Askham Bryan College wouldn't take you on straight after school. You had to get 12 months' farming experience first, so I worked on the farm where my dad worked for Robin Midgley at Manor Farm in Wigginton. One day per week I had to go to the college's out-centre at Easingwold School for what they called the pre-OND course. It's so different now. You leave school and go straight to college.

I loved it. The muck, the shit and the blather, the animals – the 40 dairy cows was the main part of Robin Midgley farm's income. My job in the winter was to muck them out using a barrow. I remember getting on the tractor in the pouring rain. It was a Massey 135 and didn't have a cab. If it was cold you got cold. If it was wet you got wet. I had to go rotovating no matter what the weather and if it was pouring down you put on a top coat and a hat and got wet.

I've always been a stock man, that's animals to those who don't know. I could never understand, and still can't, how somebody can go and sit on a tractor all day ploughing a field or rotovating and think this is wonderful. I would do it for an hour and think this is great, but then I'd be bored out of my mind, but I love stock.

I love working with animals and always have. I can still remember one or two individual cows from Mr Midgley's dairy herd.

Another job I loved was to walk the cows out of the yard after they had finished milking, down a track called Sandy Lane and into the field to graze.

My hours were 7.30 in the morning until 5 o'clock in the afternoon with an hour for lunch. I'd go home at midday with Dad. Mum would make us mashed potatoes, meat, vegetables and gravy followed by either treacle sponge pudding, treacle tart, chocolate pudding or apple pie. How we ate all that at 12 o'clock and then ate again at tea time around 5.30 I just don't know. When it was a youth club night we would also call in at the chippy and get fish and chips!

Grandad, Bob Jeffery, passed away in October 1974. I remember Nana taking me to see him just after he died in hospital. There was just me and her with him. He was the first person that I had been close to that had gone. He'd had a stroke shortly after they had moved into the bungalow after leaving Oak Lea Farm and he had struggled to walk and talk since. He was in his early 80s and I remember thinking he would be reunited with his Shire horses he loved so much.

I loved Nana and Grandad both with all my heart and still miss them now. They worked so hard to give a good foundation for all of us and I will be forever thankful for them.

I earned £13 a week working for Mr Midgley and it set me on my way for becoming Farmer Chris many years later, and I probably wouldn't have done any of what I've done since without the love of my nana and grandad and that of my mum and dad, but just for now hold on to your hats. This is when someone major comes into my life.

CHAPTER 7

The girl from Northern Ireland
My Ford Capri Mk I
From Oak Lea Farm to Scriven House Farm
Ann and a problem with Johnnie
The Norfolk Broads

Something quite major happened on Boxing Day 1974, but before we get there here's how it all came about.

Lyle's dad had married Jeanie from Northern Ireland, many years previously of course, and one of his cousins had come over to stay in the summer of 1974. She was called Sharon and she fell in love with Rob (Dent) – and me! Sharon was a very nice, accommodating party fun girl and went to Cat's Whiskers with us. We all had a lot of fun, she took lots of photographs of us, and then went back home.

Sharon's best friend back home in Northern Ireland was a girl called Donna who saw a picture of this very handsome young man and this was the start of an extraordinary part of my life. These were the times when there were massive problems not just in Northern Ireland, but also in York.

Those who remember this period will recall that Northern Ireland was at the height of its troubles and was always on the news about people being slaughtered. It was just awful, a very bad picture. Bombs had gone off at the barracks in Strensall, not far from Wigginton.

Donna had written to me, after seeing my photograph, and we had started writing to each other and telephoning. We decided we would like to meet. I wanted Donna to stay with us, my family, as Sharon and Donna were coming over together. I was quite frightened to tell them she was coming and when I announced that she was to stay with us, the day before she came, at the Christmas Day dinner table, Dad went berserk!

I'll never forget this. My dad, as calm a person as he was, hit the table with such force with his fists that all the knives and forks jumped off, and he said, 'There'll be no bloody Irish staying in this house.' Bang, that was it.

He hated what was going on and there was I wanting this young girl from Northern Ireland to stay. He was very worried that I was bringing somebody into our home who could potentially cause our family a lot of trouble. I have no idea why he thought there would be trouble but that's how he felt. He was most upset and put out by it. The outcome was that Donna could not stay with us at Oak Lea Farm, so we had to swiftly find her alternative accommodation.

On Boxing Day 1974 Rob, Stuart, Lyle and I went to Darwen in Lancashire to pick up Donna and Sharon. They'd come over on the ferry and we'd arranged to meet them at Sharon's relatives in the town. They'd picked them up from the ferry. It was late when we arrived in a Hillman Minx estate. It was terrible weather and we'd got lost on the way.

We had never met before. We had spoken on the phone. It was like love at first sight for both of us and we sat in the back smooching and cuddling with a blanket over us as we came back to Wigginton.

Donna and Sharon stayed with my Uncle John and Auntie Wendy. They had a caravan in their garden a little further up the village.

We fell in love. She was wonderful and I was absolutely smitten, more than I had been with Shelley. She was only over for a few days around Christmastime, but when it was time for her to go back, oh God it was awful. The Three Degrees' song 'When Will I See You Again?' was around at the time. That's how I felt and the words at the end of Mud's Christmas song that year 'Lonely This Christmas' – 'Merry Christmas darling, wherever you are' – were just right when she left.

But Christmas 1974 will always remain special. We had a wonderful time and she brought with her a different culture into my life. Rob was seeing Sharon, Donna and I were together and both Stuart and Lyle had girlfriends so we all went to the village dance in Huby and to Cat's Whiskers in York. We had a really nice time. Donna stayed about 5 or 6 nights. Looking back it was a brave thing for her to do and for her parents to let her come all that way to somebody she had never met before.

We kept in touch. I'd go to the telephone box in the village outside The Black Horse on a Sunday and would take £1 with me in 10p pieces. We'd have an hour on the phone. There were no mobile phones, Facebook, the internet – and I'm now 17, but I'm not ready to settle down yet. I'm sure Donna wasn't either. We'd had a lovely time, off she went back across the Irish Sea and we kept in touch.

I passed my driving test second time around in the early part of 1975 and Dad had bought me a very steady thing – an Austin 1100. I was devastated! How could I be devastated when Mum and Dad had bought me a car for goodness' sake, but I was. It was an old man's car. My mates were running around in cars like a Ford Escort or Ford Corsair, but at least I was mobile.

As soon as I could, I changed the Austin for a Ford Capri Mk I. It was the most wonderful thing I'd ever owned in my life. I'd always wanted one. It started off as brown but luckily for me, the way things worked out, someone ran into me. It was entirely their fault. Ice, they couldn't brake, and they slipped straight into the wing, which needed replacing and their insurance company was paying. It was quite a minor thing, nobody was hurt.

Geoff Nurse had the local garage in Haxby. He was a body shop repairman and I asked while it was in, could he spray it black. I had a 'Go Faster' gold stripe put down each side, those louvre black window things on the back window and a couple of spotlights. Aah! When it came out of Geoff's garage it was the dog's bollocks. You should have seen it. What a beautiful thing. Gleaming, shiny and black. I was made up with it.

So, Farmer Chris is now mobile everybody, watch out! We were by now all mobile, myself, Rob, Stuart and Lyle. We all had cassette players fitted, but Stuart had an 8-track cartridge. Wow! This was a bit more sophisticated than an ordinary cassette player. Cars didn't come with factory-fitted cassette players or 8-track cartridges in those days. If you were lucky there might have been a radio, which invariably didn't work very well.

Buying and fitting a cassette player without fusing everything else in the car became a big part of our lives, and of course the more speakers you had the better. These were really fab days of great music, which I still listen to today. Stuart loved T. Rex as we all did and all of what was called Glam Rock, as well as disco like 'Do The Hustle' by Van McCoy. Very occasionally today, I will go to Flares, which is a 70s club in York, which brings the memories flooding back.

We didn't have a lot of money, but we were all working and all had cars and our music – and the girls.

Spring 1975 brought about another move for the Jeffery family when Dad bought Scriven House Farm on the outskirts of the village. A bit like I've done at Spring View Farm at Thornton on the Hill with Kate, Dad wanted some acreage of his own as there was no land as such at Oak Lea. It was for sale through Stephensons who also run the York Auction Centre livestock market in Murton near York.

We'd only been at Oak Lea for three years, but with just a house, buildings and maybe a field at the back; and Wigginton continually being developed with more housing he had set his heart on Scriven House when it came up.

The fly in the ointment, as Dad saw it, was that Robin Midgley also wanted to buy it, but fortunately for Dad Robin couldn't raise the funds.

On the morning of the sale Dad and I were working one of Robin's fields pulling sugar beet or something or other and Dad just said, 'Right, I'm off,' and he turned around as he was leaving and said, 'It'll be mine.' And off he went with Mum to Murton. They came home that night and they had bought it, farmhouse, farm buildings and 28 acres for £18,200. We moved shortly after.

I met Ann in 1975. Ann from Husthwaite. We'd met in a pub in Easingwold. She was a lovely, very slim attractive young lady with short brown hair. She was a hairdresser and had a Triumph Herald. We had petted, snogged and had a few nice times in the car, but we'd never gone the full way. I was still a virgin.

That summer Mum and Dad went on holiday again to Ilfracombe with my brothers to see Aunt Ellen. They wanted me to stay at their new home, to look after the farm as by now Dad had cattle and pigs on the farm. He'd buy store bullocks and weaned pigs taking them on to finishing. He used to mill and mix his own livestock feed too. Having the run of the place to myself was fine by me!

I told Ann my mum and dad were going away and I

had the house to myself. That Saturday night we went to a barn dance in the village, but we both knew where we really wanted to be. We were at the dance for about an hour before coming back home and the plan was that Ann was going to stay the night. I was so excited. I had my own room with a single bed, but I'd thought this was no bloody good – I need to have my first experience in a double bed. I lost my virginity to Ann that night in my parents' bed! How did I dare do that? Sorry Mum!

Something happened that was quite hilarious though. I'd been practising putting a 'johnnie' on all week because I'd never used one and what happened? Let's just say I was a bit previous! But in those days 15 minutes later I was ready again, and off we went!

My second lads holiday was with Rob, Stuart and Lyle. We booked a motor cruiser on the Norfolk Broads. We'd never driven a boat before – I think that should be steered – and we should never have been allowed on it. It was ridiculous. First of all we crashed into the side of the bank head on and got stuck and then when we used the little motor boat we'd hired with it, we lost the outboard motor off it, which sank. One of us, it can't have been me, had to go into the river or canal to pull it out, but it was broken. Rob managed to mend it with a tin opener, don't ask me how.

This was when we'd all decided, on the way down, to have an alter-ego for all the women we were going to delight. Rob decided on his new name as we went through a village in Lincolnshire. He became Richard Fosdyke – and as we went over a bridge approaching the Broads it reminded me of a smaller version of the Sydney Harbour Bridge, so I decided I would call myself Sidney Mooring, as I saw a boat moored nearby.

Can you believe, people still call me Sid today? I have some who have known me as nothing else but Sid for nearly 50 years! I didn't aim to keep the name, but still today I get people come into the shop saying, 'All right, Sid?'. It all goes back to 1975.

When we moored up in Great Yarmouth there were that many boats we had to walk across others to get to the land. This was where we went to watch my first X-rated sex movie. Stuart tells me it was *Eskimo Nell*. It was also known as *The Sexy Saga of Naughty Nell & Big Dick*, apparently! I wouldn't know, but in the course of our research we found that Christopher Timothy (*All Creatures Great & Small*) and Christopher Biggins were in it. Anyway, we were all sat there smoking, as you could, and decided we would have a bit of fun with Rob.

You could get these bangers that you pushed into the end of a cigarette and after a couple of drags would blow up.

So, we're all sat there, intent on this sex film, but watching out for when Rob's cigarette blew and all of a sudden it did! We were quickly thrown out. I think they got more of a bang than they expected that day!

Worse news was to follow. By the time we got back to the boat the tide had gone out, so ours was a bit further down than we might have expected. We jumped on to this other man's boat that we were moored next to at 1 in the morning and caused all kind of fuss when we started up the battery to cook some eggs. There was hell on! We caused mayhem that night, starting the engine and having our music blaring, but we were four teenage lads on a boat. No wonder they don't allow that kind of thing these days!

And things were only going to get worse! The next day we set off across Breydon Water. It is now the UK's largest protected wetland and is known as the Gateway to The Broads. Stuart, Rob and I were all talking downstairs when we realised Lyle was down with us too. Four out of four of us – and all down below! That's when we suddenly thought, 'Who the hell is driving the boat?' and the answer of course was nobody! We're all in this kitchen area and there was nothing up top, a bit like us!

We had a really fun time on the boat, but we were also pretty irresponsible. You just don't allow lads like us to do that anymore – and I for one can see why! Other than the water I have to tell you it was a pretty dry week on the woman front, but we had a great time!

CHAPTER 8

The College Years

September 1975 and I am finally starting my college studies at Askham Bryan College. It's situated just a handful of miles west of York. All I'd ever wanted to do was to go into farming. Mum was disappointed. She'd been hoping that with going to a grammar school I would do well academically, but that was never going to be. I think she'd thought maybe I might become a solicitor or accountant, but it was Mum who had also said if I wanted to get into farming I should do it properly and go to college.

I'd said I didn't want to go, but had gone for the interview, which you had to do back then. But in 1974 when I'd gone for the initial interview I'd then taken up my 12 months with Robin Midgley and now that was completed I was here, safely delivered courtesy of my Ford Capri and ready to embark on my three-year Ordinary National Diploma in Agriculture. Ordinary! I hate that name for it, fancy calling it that!

I took to college life, really enjoyed it and made some good friends. I was living-in in student accommodation on the college campus. The accommodation and the food was quite basic, but there was a student bar that we all took turns to run and the beer was cheap. We'd go to the pubs in the villages of Askham Bryan and Askham Richard too.

The course was full-on and that first year we were working from 9 in the morning until 5 at night for 5 days in seminars and studies, except Wednesday afternoon, which was sports afternoon and I played rugby for the college team. Wednesday night teas after our game were fantastic – eggs, chips and beans with bread and butter followed by rice pudding or something equally good. It was our favourite tea of the week – dinner to all you *Celebs on the Farm* southerners!

Typically, with loads of lads together all in our teens, we got up to some naughty tricks and one of them was on the college vice principal Brian Thomas who was a complete and utter bastard, so he deserved it. We all hated him.

Big round bales of straw were just becoming all the rage at the time and one night we decided it would be quite fun to roll one down the campus and then roll the whole bale out on the vice principal's lawn. If you had seen his lawn you would know how beautiful it was and it was kept in pristine condition. The grass was like bowling green quality. There was no CCTV in those days, no security cameras. The next morning Mr Thomas would get up and see his carefully manicured lawn covered in a carpet of rolled barley straw, but like I said, he was a dick so he deserved everything he had coming to him so far as we were concerned.

Another one of our lads' japes was quite dangerous when I think about it now and totally irresponsible. The old entrance to the college's main building had a long, majestic driveway direct from the A64, but because of the huge amount of traffic now on this very busy road that connects Leeds and the A1 with York, Malton, Pickering and Scarborough, it had long since been replaced by a new entrance where you have to come off the main road less than a quarter of a mile further up and towards the village of Askham Bryan, much safer. The gates to the old entrance were now permanently closed – or they were until we had our idea.

Again at night-time we decided to open the gates and we put up a big sign at the side of the A64 saying 'Transport

Café'. Well, my God, all these cars and trucks were coming up the bloody drive, just as we'd hoped, and because there were so many there was nowhere to turn around – and of course no transport café! Oh how we laughed! Another problem for Mr Thomas!

It was also never a good idea for anyone to go home for a weekend, because when you came back you were never quite sure what would have happened to your room and your belongings. As I mentioned the accommodation was fairly basic. The rooms were tiny – you had a bed, a sink, a wardrobe and a cupboard.

The doors were quite easy to take off and we found it great fun, if somebody was away, to take off their door, take everything out of their room and put it in the garden, literally everything – bed, bedding, all possessions – clothes, books, records, girlie mags, johnnies, beer, the lot!

This poor guy, whoever our victim was, would come back on the Sunday night, try to open his door and it would just fall off. Didn't we get up to some awful things! Once again, this time *Celebs on the Farm* people – never try this on our show. Just saying.

During the first year of our course we had to decide on which area of farming we wanted to specialize in our third year, as the second year was to be spent on placement on farms where we would be employed as students. In your first year you study a broad cross-section of agriculture, but the second year is meant to start focusing you on where you are likely to end up in employment.

One guy who helped me a lot through college was Bernard Ashworth. Bernard was a lovely chap who, as well as being a tutor, was responsible for helping us decide which specialist area we would choose and placing us on appropriate farms in our middle year. Later in my life Bernard also helped me with something that won me an award. Sadly he's no longer with us.

I chose pigs. I chose this sector because I liked animals, but also because I felt there would be an opportunity of a good job at the end of it. I didn't want to drive tractors as I found that too boring and I didn't fancy dairy cows. I could have gone with beef cattle or sheep but went with pigs as I felt the wages for a pig unit manager would be better than other livestock.

Pigs, as we all know in farming, have always been up and down, quite a volatile sector price wise, but they were making quite decent money in those days.

We had the smallest group in history as only three of us had decided to do pigs. My other two cohorts were a lad called Paul Smith and another called Dave Rawlings. Dave and I became great pals. He didn't stay in student accommodation because he only lived a handful of miles away at Wighill. He now makes his own potato vodka that we stock in our shop and runs a fabulous wedding and special event venue with great accommodation from his farm at Syningthwaite.

Around this time in my first college year on campus in 1975 I'm still seeing Ann and we were having a nice time; and I was still seeing her in my first work placement that started in June 1976. Donna would also come over from Northern Ireland whenever she could. There was a time when I always seemed to be saying goodbye to Donna on a train or an aeroplane or something. We were keeping in touch.

In those days Askham Bryan College was quite small with only around 300 students of which 297 were male. So, what happened at the end of each term, when a dance was organized in the conference hall, was all these girls from the University of York St John were bussed over! I can't quite believe it happened now, but of course we all paired up. It was like putting a load of bulls with a load of heifers. There was lots of nookie. We were students after all.

Bernard put me with a pig farmer called Wilf Davis at Newton upon Derwent about 5 miles west of the East Riding market town of Pocklington for my first 6 months and that was a real eye-opener in some ways. You used to have a day beforehand when you would go out and meet the farmer, his farm staff and find out where you were going to live. The farmer goes through what is expected of you. I recall it was a very hot day in June when I went to meet Wilf, his wife and the team.

Wilf had quite a big pig unit with about 300 sows. It was a very intensive pig farm with everything indoors on slats. All the progeny from these 300 sows were then taken through to bacon. To those who don't know, that means the piglets they gave birth to, usually around 13-14 piglets per sow twice a year, would be grown to the weight needed to go to a bacon factory, so you're talking about 8000 pigs a year going into the meat industry from Wilf's farm. He also had a small herd of Gelbvieh cattle, a German breed that were quite crazy.

Where I was going to stay, while working for Wilf was a bit of a learning curve to say the least. I wasn't very keen on it. The house was a townhouse in Pocklington. I've never been one for living in a town, but now that I think about it, we were only really there for breakfast and in the evening. We'd leave the place at 7.30 for an 8 o'clock start and we'd be back again for 5.30. It was a shared house with about 12 of us who were working on different farms. I shared a bedroom with two other guys and there was a communal toilets and shower area.

I've never been in the Armed Forces but it felt a bit like what you might imagine life is like in barracks. There was no hiding place for anything and not a lot of dignity.

This red-haired woman with glasses ran the house and

probably owned it, I don't know, but she also lived there with her son who these days would probably have been called autistic, but in those days was referred to as a bit backward.

We had a big open kitchen where we all ate together on a night and I always remember it was the first and last time I've ever eaten pigeon. It was bloody 'orrible! This woman wasn't renowned for her cooking the best of food, but she always made us a pack-up for our lunch, she washed our clothes, we always had a breakfast and we had a big room with a television and chairs. It was a bit rough and ready but served its purpose.

Coming back every day from working with pigs the one thing anyone will tell you is that you stink of them. A shower was an absolute necessity.

Working for Wilf Davis I started to learn about pigs – and people! Wilf had this most terrifying man as his pig foreman, Bill Bradley. He was the most dreadful, hard taskmaster I'd ever met in my life and another complete bastard.

Bill would shout and swear at us. I was the only student there, but there were other staff and he was the same with everyone. He was such a stickler for cleanliness on the farm. If you were power washing a farrowing house and you left one bit of muck on one of the pig crates he went utterly berserk and you had to go back in and scrub it off until it was absolutely gleaming.

Looking back now he was a fantastic mentor as well as a hard taskmaster and I took a lot of his qualities on board when I started my own business, but he was still a bastard – and a twat come to that – but by God he was good at his job, very organized and a very skilful and efficient pig man who knew his job inside out.

I ended up being Bill's best mate, because I wanted to learn and wanted to be good – and I was! He could see it too. He saw how interested I was in being the best I could be and he'd have me thrown into everything. I was helping to mate the sows and boars (my specialist subject, of course) and working on everything I could regarding pig husbandry, from looking after them to spreading pig slurry on the land.

The farm was set up with the emphasis on maximum production and we were on with Large White X Landrace hybrids that were in demand at the time. It was terrible animal welfare really. Every sow was kept in a stall all its life, everything lived on slats. I hate the thought of it now. It's not the way my Oxford Sandy & Blacks are raised I can tell you, but I had a good work experience at Wilf's farm from June until December 1976.

I would stay at the house in Pocklington through the week and come home to Wigginton at the weekend. Stuart, Rob, Lyle and I would be out on the town again, but every Wednesday night there was a disco at a pub called The Squirrels on the A1079 York-Hull road and everyone used to go, including a lot of the Pocklington girls, which spelled the end for Ann and I. I'd got a different life going on now.

Ann came over one Wednesday night and I just said, 'I'm sorry, that's it, we're finished.' I don't think I ever saw her again. She used to come all the way from Easingwold to see me and she was a really lovely girl, nice to be with and I liked her, but I just didn't love her.

In the summer of 1976 the Fab 4 were on holiday again. No boat this time, instead we went to Newquay and St Ives in Cornwall and Weston-super-Mare on the Somerset coast in an old Ford Transit van. The sleeping arrangements left a bit to be desired, or at least mine did! Three were to sleep in the van and one in the tent behind it. I was the youngest, so I went in the tent.

We'd been hoping to get to Land's End but the van

didn't make it and broke down. We mended it and just had a proper four lads on holiday. It was another dry week in terms of female company but we were having a good time camping, cooking breakfasts and generally having a laugh.

After finishing at Wilf's farm in December 1976 I was at home for Christmas before starting my second farm placement at another pig farm in the tiny village of Scackleton, which is near Hovingham in the Howardian Hills. I was to work for Rowbottom Brothers who also had another pig unit over in Patrington in Holderness near the east coast. They had a lot of arable land over there and were a much bigger farming enterprise than Wilf's. The farm at Scackleton was a 500-sow pig unit and once again with all progeny taken to bacon.

But my God, if my accommodation had been a culture shock at Pocklington it was nothing compared to the old chapel in the village that had been converted into student accommodation.

Friggin' 'ell! I arrived on this Sunday night in January 1977 and I couldn't believe what I'd come to! The door was banging away in the wind, it was dark, raining and there was just me. I put the lights on, walked into the kitchen and it just looked like a bomb had gone off. It was dreadful. It was the most dirty, smelly, horrible place. Honestly, you wouldn't have kept a dog in it, or if you had you would have been reported for cruelty to animals, it was horrible.

There were three of us in the chapel's two bedrooms. I had to share and I remember this guy called Kit had his own bedroom because he worked on the farm full-time. The other lad was a student from another college. They arrived shortly after I got there, we had a few beers, talked about the farm and started getting to know each other. I soon became accustomed to the way we were going to live but it was a dramatic experience. At least at Pocklington everything was clean and tidy and meals were prepared for us, here we were looking after ourselves and it was always a mess.

Tony Maxwell was the pig farm manager at Scackleton. He was entirely different to Bill Bradley but again was another hard taskmaster. He was very strong-willed and very particular about how he wanted things run, but he wasn't a shouter and swearer. He was very experienced, probably around 60 years old, and a very nice, hard and firm man who expected the very best from his team of 10.

Despite the chapel, as my time at Scackleton went on, I liked the whole experience better than I had when living in Pocklington, mainly because I was living in the countryside.

Once again though, the farm itself was very intensive with sows all tethered, tied up all the time, and everything on slats. I still don't like that.

Dave Fitton was the sow manager and helped me learn more about pigs and efficiency. He was a very nice chap and I enjoyed learning about pig genetics and breeding. I was already very interested in the farrowing rather than the fattening side – and how to produce as many pigs from a sow per year but doing it properly by keeping the piglet deaths to a minimum.

One quite funny but certainly embarrassing situation with my mother happened at Scriven House Farm one night after a very heavy drinking session with Rob, Lyle and Stuart. I was home from Scackleton for the weekend. The lads dropped me off at the farm after the village dance. I went upstairs to bed and at some point I got up to go to the loo. I turned the wrong way out of the bedroom and the world disappeared beneath me!

I had fallen down the stairs, rolled into the front door and wet myself on the carpet! To make matters worse I was naked! Mum heard the noise, came down and found me in pain and worse for wear. She managed to get me back into bed and left me in disgust. The next morning I awoke with pains in my head, wrist and ankle. I dragged myself downstairs not knowing what had happened. Mum looked at me in disgust again and looked about to chastise me, but could see I was in agony.

I had to go to casualty as I couldn't walk. My wrist and ankle were sprained and I couldn't go back to work the following week. Tony (Maxwell) was most displeased and I was worried this may impact on my college result. I ate a lot of humble pie and to win him over I spent the springtime tidying the garden at the old chapel which pleased him immensely. Thankfully he didn't report the incident to the college.

The chapel also had its uses as Donna came over at some point while I was at Scackleton and that's where we first slept together. The lad who shared with me had cleared off by then. I had another visitor too, as Bernard (Ashworth) would come out and see me from time to time on both farms. I finished at Scackleton in June 1977.

By now, having gained what was really valuable experience, I could see where I was heading. I wanted to be in charge of a pig unit when I finished college, because I felt very capable of producing good figures and that was what it was all about, getting the maximum amount of pigs per sow per year, which means getting as much meat as possible from a sow. At that time the maximum amount of pigs produced per year from a sow was 24. It's now over 30. Sows have 2.56 litters per year. If you have 500 sows that's up to 15,000 pigs for bacon.

I was really confident in my ability with pigs and enjoyed working with them. In September 1977 I returned to Askham Bryan College for my third year and was living-in again on campus, but this time in nicer accommodation in a new block they'd built, with doors that could not be removed! This was a lovely room and I think I even had my own loo!

Dave, Paul and I, being in a group of just three, pretty much had our own personal tutor who had an old Russian Moskvitch car and every week we would visit a pig unit to see how pigs were kept in different ways. These were very different days when pigs were often fed on pig swill – which is kitchen waste, scraps that could contain any kind of meat. It was pig swill at a farm in the North East that was said to be the cause of the Foot and Mouth epidemic in 2001. Bloody awful. Pigs were being fed on everything without any thought for what they were eating. Oh dear me, but it was happening then when we were students.

Our tutor was really good with us and a thoroughly nice chap. As well as specializing in pigs we also did chemistry, which I hated; land management, beef and sheep husbandry, accounts and other subjects that fitted for our OND qualification. We had to obtain a pass in everything. You had to have sufficient good reports from your employers in the middle year, prepare a project and pass the final exams that would be sat in May 1978, but my world changed massively in that 12 months from September 1977 to August 1978. Maybe it was all down to Donna (Summer) singing 'I Feel Love' that summer in 1977, but my world seemed to come together, happily.

CHAPTER 9

Donna

Something quite scary happens in 1977. Donna and I are getting very close. I made several trips over to Northern Ireland over this period. I'd still had girls I'd seen and remember seeing a girl who was an occupational therapist in York. We had a wild time, but we were just being students. But Donna and I were getting to know each other a bit more and maybe I was deciding I'd sown enough wild oats.

It hadn't been like I was ever cheating on Donna, our relationship wasn't like that. We both knew what we were doing. We had wanted to keep in touch with each other, but I think we both knew there were other people along the way.

But now things were getting serious. I must have been over to Northern Ireland about ten times in my Ford Capri. I can't believe I did that. It was about 240 miles from Wigginton to Stranraer and took the best part of 6 hours and then 2 hours on the ferry, then up the coast to her parents' house. Back then the road network was pretty much one road from when you came off the M6 and took you through all of the towns like Gatehouse of Fleet and Dumfries. It took forever. The ferry went to Larne in County Antrim where Donna and her brother Robert would meet me.

Northern Ireland was a terrible place to be because of the bombings and shootings but it was and still is a beautiful place with lovely people.

Donna's family lived in a 3-bedroomed mid-terraced

house in Whitehead near Carrickfergus in County Antrim. It was a truly beautiful, quite small, old Victorian seaside town that had seen better days and was a bit run down on account of nobody going on holiday there anymore. It's where Bill Cass, Lyle's dad, met Jeanie his wife when he was on holiday years before.

I'd stay with them for sometimes a week, maybe more, particularly in Summer 1977. There was her mum and dad Betty and Donny Wilson and her brother Robert. I slept in a single bed in Robert's room. Donna was in her room. Donny worked at the big Kilroot power station. He was a lovely, great big, strong Protestant Irish man who was fiercely proud. He lived for Betty, and as long as she was happy so was he.

Robert was very religious and was also a church organist. He had a very good job as appeals director for Barnardo's. When I was over I'd spend a day or two with him and he'd go around the whole country collecting Barnardo's boxes from pubs and clubs. Donna was at work at the time, so I'd get to see a lot more of Northern Ireland and of places where we shouldn't really have been, like the Falls Road and Shankill Road. He was very naughty. It didn't bother him about the Troubles. I guess he just saw it as part of their lives, but I was scared.

He showed me all around Belfast. Buses turned over on fire, massive corrugated gates between streets. I saw it all up close and the army with all the guns, the patrols. Everywhere you went you were stopped by them. Schools were surrounded with barbed wire, all the pubs had mesh over the windows, concrete barrels all around and masses of checkpoints.

Whitehead is sixteen and a half miles north east of Belfast and a very nice part of the world. The promenade running from Whitehead to Blackhead was okay to walk and so we did.

Their social life involved a totally different culture to what I had been used to and I liked it, so I did! They introduced me to something I'd never experienced before! Wait for it! You're going to be stunned!

They used to go out for tea! What the hell was that all about? I'm a Yorkshire farmer's son. I don't go out for tea! They'd say let's go out for tea tonight at the golf club. So, off we'd go and before tea we'd had maybe three or four gin and tonics!

Out for tea, for goodness' sake! We never went out for tea and Dad rarely drank at home, apart from on a Sunday when he might go down to the Black Horse and buy himself a bottle of brown ale, Mum a Babycham and me a pineapple juice or something.

Donny was so proud of Donna and spoilt her rotten. Whatever she wanted, she got from him, but he was also delighted his daughter had found a big strapping Yorkshire farmer. Yes, she was a very spoilt child and if she didn't get her own way there was hell to pay, but I loved her.

That Summer of 1977 we got engaged while I was in Whitehead. We both just wanted to do it, we were that much in love with each other.

When you look back at it now, you think, 'Good God! How did you know your own mind?' I was 19 and Donna was 18. We were just kids. Her brother Robert was so excited because all he could think about was organising the most wonderful wedding. So, I'm going back for my final year at Askham Bryan College, engaged to Donna.

I didn't get on particularly well with my mum from around 17-25 years old and I'm not totally sure why. Maybe it was because I had spent so much time with Nana from an early age while Mum was in hospital. It was an effort for us to speak nicely to each other in this period and she certainly didn't think Donna was right for me.

She thought I was totally bonkers getting engaged and married at such an early age and she was probably right in hindsight. She was, however, and still is, an extremely kind, loving and caring mother who only wants the best for me, my brothers and all our families.

In the Spring of 1978 Donna and I decided that she should come and live with us at Scriven House Farm in Wigginton. Dad must have come round to the idea of allowing Donna in our house by now. Donna's parents came over to see where their daughter was going to stay. This was a major thing, letting her daughter go to live in England. There were tears already, in that first week when Donny and Betty came, before Donna was even staying at the farm. They idolized her.

I decided to live at home now and commute to college in the final weeks of my time before the exams. Donna took a secretarial job in York and we were officially an item. I did my final exams and qualified. You do your exams in April/May and suddenly college life is over.

Getting a job was top of my agenda, especially now I was getting married. Bernard tried to help us all find jobs, but could I hell as find anything. I didn't expect to get a manager's job straight away, but maybe an assistant manager's. Eventually I found this job as assistant pig man to the manager of a traditional pig unit in a village called Hengrave near Bury St Edmunds in Suffolk! Crikey!

It wasn't as intensive as the pig farms I'd worked at during college, as most of the sows were in yards, which was lovely, and some were outside as well, even better. The company was called Abingdon Farms Ltd and the big attraction for someone about to get married was that it came with a bungalow. I thought I'd cracked it if they offered me the job. Somewhere to live, we had wheels and I thought it might be nice for Donna since she had moved from her family in Northern Ireland that I had left mine too. We would be somewhere totally new to us both and starting out on our own.

The farm was also in a heartland of the pig sector and maybe it would be good for my career. I got the job and started in June 1978. Donna went back to Northern Ireland to prepare for the wedding and I set about decorating this bungalow that came with the job and had a nice garden.

I'd never decorated before but all of a sudden I'm putting woodchip all over the walls. In the first month I'd decorated the whole bungalow for my bride. I travelled up to York and then Stranraer to catch the ferry so that I could stay with Donny and Betty Wilson and their beautiful daughter.

We were married in St Patrick's Church in Jordanstown, 10 miles down the coast from Whitehead on 26 August 1978. It was the church where Robert was the organist and he organised the whole wedding, he was a brilliant organiser.

All my family and friends were there. They'd all made the journey and I know everyone from my side was quite fearful because of where they were staying with all the Troubles and the bombs, but everyone enjoyed the wedding and the reception at Ballygally Castle Hotel just north of Larne, that Donna and I travelled to in a white Rolls Royce.

My mother's mother, who was in her late 80s, travelled over and everyone went over via Stranraer. The boys were all there and Rob (Dent) was best man. I'll never forget in church at the font, Rob looked at me and said, 'Hey, come on, this is our one chance here. Let's get out and go.'

It was a lovely day and a fantastic wedding. The weather was beautiful and we stayed overnight in the hotel. On the Sunday we started our honeymoon for two nights in a hotel in Keswick in the Lake District and it pissed it down. We'd planned three or four nights in the

Lakes, but the weather and Donna being so keen for us to get to our own new place meant we cut it short.

By now the Ford Capri had gone. I must have sold it to help fund the wedding ring. We now had an old dark brown (urgh) and rusty Ford Cortina. I loved that Ford Capri.

Donna loved nice things. Her mum and dad didn't have a big house but they had a lovely carpet, nice furniture and furnishings. I'd done everything I could to make the bungalow a lovely place to come to. When we moved in everything was new and fresh. We had this log burning stove and Dad had bought us a brand-new chainsaw as a wedding present for cutting logs. I was always getting logs together.

This extremely attractive, very sexy, amazingly lovely loving girl and loving person who I loved everything about, from her shapeliness, naturally dark hair to her sultry Irish accent, is the only person in my life that I have felt I could look into her eyes and see into her soul.

CHAPTER 10

My Two Little Boys

Donna and I had things going really well for the first few months. Yes, months, but it wasn't that there was anything wrong between us at the time. I'd started work on the farm and was enjoying the job and Donna had started working in the lovely farm shop on the site.

Donny became very ill. He had stomach cancer and took ill shortly after we married. We didn't know how serious it was at first, but he had to undergo quite a lot of treatment, as you might expect, and ended up having a major operation where they removed his stomach by basically cutting him in half. He showed me the scar when he, Betty and Robert stayed with us a while, but they didn't have the technology they have now and he was about to get even worse.

So, now we're two young kids of 20 and 19, many miles from both our family homes, with no real friends around us. Donna is homesick. Her dad's poorly. We have no social life. We don't go out anywhere and the car, that bloody awful rusty Ford Cortina, got us to Bury St Edmunds and then just collapsed.

We scrapped the car. Donna went on the bus into town for any shopping she wanted, and we did get to know our neighbours, my manager John and his lovely American wife Mary, but things weren't feeling right. We spent our first Christmas as man and wife on our own. It was quite distressing. We'd always been used to having family around.

In the New Year of 1979 Donna announced she was

pregnant. I couldn't believe it and I wasn't happy about it. We had talked about having children and we weren't going to have any at that time. Donna was on the pill, or so I'd thought. Looking back I think it was Donna's cry for help: 'Look at me, I'm homesick and I need some help.' I was quite cross at the time. I said, 'I don't want you to be pregnant, we're too young,' but there wasn't a lot I could do. We were starting a family.

But that wasn't all. Donny was getting progressively worse and in May 1979 we went over to Northern Ireland via York and Stranraer. We had bought a yellow Hillman Avenger automatic for £200 and when we arrived he was in intensive care. He had been a very big, strong man and now he was a skeleton and was clearly going to die. I knew I had to be back at work so I stayed a week and then left Donna there with her mum and brother. I made the long haul back to Bury St Edmunds via the ferry, Stranraer and York.

The minute I arrived back at the farm in Bury St Edmunds, my neighbour John came out from next door and said, 'Chris, you're going to have to go back, your father-in-law has died.' I had a cup of tea, got back in the car and drove back to York. Mum and Dad paid for me to fly from Leeds-Bradford airport to Belfast airport. Betty had relied on Donny so much that I had no idea how things were going to turn out.

My employers Abingdon Farms were very good and gave me compassionate leave while I stayed in Northern Ireland supporting Donna. It was a terrible time. Robert organized the funeral, which was held very quickly, unlike these days where they seem to take ages.

I flew back after the funeral leaving Donna to grieve with and support her mum and brother. When Donna came back Betty came with her and stayed with us for a while.

Farming, Celebs and Plum Pudding Pigs!

We made our next move in July 1979. As we had a baby on the way we felt we needed to be nearer family, people that we knew. We were too remote from family where we were, so I wrote to my previous employer Wilf Davis at Newton-upon-Derwent telling him I was looking for a job. I'd heard on the grapevine that Bill Bradley, my mentor, had left. I got his job, and it came with a lovely bungalow too. We hired a van and moved back to Yorkshire. Result!

It was a shame about having to leave Hengrave because I really enjoyed living there and it was a traditional, old-fashioned farm. I loved the way they kept the pigs. I'd only been there just over a year and Donna just under a year, but circumstances were against us.

We moved everything ourselves. First we came to Newton-upon-Derwent in the van, then I drove back down to Bury St Edmunds and came back in the Hillman Avenger, all in the same day. As it turned out the move didn't make a lot of difference because we hardly saw any of my friends and family at the time. Betty came over though, to be with her daughter.

Summer 1979 was also a major moment – for my dad!

Dad's accident changed Mum and Dad's life. He was baling straw for Robin Midgley and foolishly got off the tractor, with the engine and baler still in motion, to try and unblock it. This next part is not pretty.

At the point he put his arm in the baler it 'tripped' and the needles came up with huge force in the baler's chamber.

Dad's arm was mangled. How he managed to stagger from the field to the farmhouse is a miracle. He was in such pain. He was taken to York District Hospital where they operated on him immediately. His arm was in a terrible state and it was only because of the wonderful surgeons that his arm was saved.

This finished Dad's work in farming. He was disabled

and for a year afterwards unable to use his arm, so he couldn't work. He went to rehabilitation and eventually got a job as a gardener and handyman at a disabled children's home in York – St Monica's & St Hilda's. He got back partial use of his arm and was able to drive and do this sort of work well. It changed him so much for he better as he was involved with workmates, mostly women, for the first time ever!

He loved it, especially as the women used to tease him and he responded to it with great enthusiasm. Mum loved it that he was out of farming with all of its long hours and sometimes long and demanding work. He was there some fifteen years and retired with a nice pension.

Robert was born at Fulford Maternity Hospital, York on 22 September 1979. I'm 21 and Donna is 20. Donna had a long labour. She started in the morning and it was nearly 24 hours later, just as they were going to use forceps that Rob was born. I remember his head was shaped like an egg and at first I thought he was deformed, but he was fine. Donna said, 'Has he got all his little fingers and tootsies?'

Donna and I were still in love, but it was also a hard time with her dad having died, Donna being homesick, no friends around, no social life and having no real savings, just living day by day – and now we had a child.

And this child was the most awful damned child you could wish for! He never slept! God, it was hard rearing Rob. Donna and I would take it in turns to walk the floor with him on a night, cradling him until he went off – and the minute you put him down in his cot he'd start again.

Donna's mum stayed quite some time to help when Rob was born. Betty was a great help.

And within a year, would you believe it, we had two sons! Donna tried to breast feed Robert but he wouldn't take it. She was then told she was short of iron and the district nurse would come and give her this massive injection of iron into her bum, bless her. But what we really hadn't expected was for the district nurse to announce, just a few weeks after Rob had been born that the good news was Robert was nice and healthy – and the other news was Donna was pregnant again!

What I can tell you is, for all of our troubles, Donna and I had a very passionate relationship – and good old Farmer Chris had definitely been back in the saddle very quickly.

David was born at Fulford Maternity Hospital August 7, 1980. He was a lovely, healthy little boy and a lot nicer as a baby than Rob had been. He slept! We'd both been terrified of having another baby like Rob who'd been difficult to get off to sleep. We'd had Rob christened in Northern Ireland earlier that year.

One of the most wonderful experiences of my life has been to be with my wife both times as she gave birth. Just amazing moments. Me, Donna and our two sons.

But we're still not happy. Donna's certainly not happy. She wants to be back in Ireland. Her father's gone, her mother's lost without Donny and Donna. And my mum and dad don't really approve of Donna. Mum certainly never thought Donna was good enough for me, but now there are grandsons. It's all a mess and my mind was in turmoil.

We had to do something because Donna and her mother were now in a terrible state. The power of all these emotions became so strong that we made the decision to move to Northern Ireland in October 1980.

I gave up my life as a pig farmer, something I'd spent my life working towards, and we moved lock, stock and barrel to Whitehead in Co Antrim. I was trying my best to do the right thing by my wife.

Donna flew over with the children. We hired a man

and a van and I travelled with him with all our stuff to Stranraer and over the Irish Sea. We'd been fortunate to find a man who was going back home himself.

My time in Northern Ireland didn't last long at all. I managed to get a job working with pigs, but it was a small run-down unit and all of the pigs had rhinitis. He wanted me to get rid of this disease and to set it up as a breeding unit. He had a concrete factory making concrete blocks in Carrowdore in Co Down.

The owner was like some kind of gangster businessman with a big Jaguar car and I remember being in it one day when he opened the glove compartment and revealed a gun! He said he carried it with him all the time. I think he was a Catholic.

It turned out he was a very wealthy, well-known character and in those days the paramilitary would abduct people like him and set up a ransom figure. It really was a sign of the times.

Donna and I, Rob and David, both less than 2 years old, were living with Betty and Robert until just before Christmas when we began renting this really horrible terraced house. Betty got us it through where she worked part-time in a DIY shop. The guy who had the shop also owned the house we moved into. It was basic with no garden, just a back yard, but at least it was somewhere we were on our own. My pay from the job was rubbish but it got us a bit of income and I managed to buy a little bubble car for a couple of hundred quid. But my job didn't last.

This is where the whole thing turned on its head. Donna was the one who ended up with a job working with Robert at Barnardo's and I'm now in this bloody place as a house husband in Northern Ireland. I'm looking after our two little boys. I'm feeding them breakfast, taking them for a walk, doing the shopping. I've one baby in the pram and the other on a seat on the pram.

I'm walking down the road one day and I'm thinking what the hell am I doing? I was making a life for us in England. We had lovely nice bungalows in Bury St Edmunds and Newton-upon-Derwent with lovely gardens. And now I didn't have a job and Donna did. That's when I started to believe Donna had used all of what had happened to get me over here under false pretences.

Mum came over for my 23rd birthday in 1981, saw where I was living, talked with me and could see it just wasn't working out. She said, 'Chris, what are you doing?' and I thought, yeah, I don't know what I'm doing.

In February 1981, I said to Donna, 'I'm going home. I can't be here anymore. I can't be a house husband. I can't do this. You either come with me or you don't, but I'm going home.'

I certainly wouldn't have said it as rationally as all that. We would both have 'effed and jeffed'. There was nothing calm and rational about me and Donna. We fought like cat and dog at times. When things were good they were very, very good, but when they were bad and she didn't get her own way, wow, did you know about it. She had one fiery Irish temper. Our conversation more likely ended with a verbal spat from both of us and Donna said, 'Go and f*** off back to York then.' Her mother knew what she was like and once said to me, 'Chris, I don't know how you live with my daughter.'

Donna moved back in with her mother and brother with our boys and that was it, the end of our marriage. Christ! Two and a half years, four homes, two little boys, three jobs and I was going home with nothing! I flew home, leaving my wife, my children – I still can't believe I left my children. I loved them, but I left them. That was it. Marriage over.

CHAPTER 11

Diane and Donna

I'd known the Plowman family for years. They were livestock and meat hauliers between Wigginton and Sutton on the Forest and are still there now. It was Dave Plowman who gave me my first job when I returned home to Scriven House Farm from Northern Ireland.

Dick Plowman was Dave's son and came with me on my first trips out with the lorry delivering meat. He was only a young lad but clearly had the potential to take over his dad's business in the future. He and his brother Matt now run the very successful Plowman business near Wigginton manufacturing livestock lorry bodies.

Dave had a fleet of lorries and employed drivers and my job was driving a 7.5 tonne meat lorry, collecting huge sides of beef from Alf Mead's abattoir (it's now ABP) in Murton next to the livestock market and driving the meat to local butchers. My job was humping! Humping meat!

I wasn't just driving. I had to be at the abattoir for 3 o'clock in the morning to help load all the big articulated transport that was taking beef sides down to Smithfield market and all over the UK. The heaviest meat I ever carried on my shoulder was a forequarter of a bull that weighed 23 stones.

I carried it in to the Co-op in Malton. I was a very fit, strong young man. There were two forequarters to be unloaded and this first one I dropped off the hook in my lorry, grabbed it, hauled it on to my right shoulder, staggered in and dropped it on the butcher's block. I said he'd have to come out and cut the other one up in the truck. Now that's proper humping for you!

Dave was their transport manager and I was contracted to drive this much smaller wagon that could be driven on a car driving licence. My lorry was always last to be loaded as I was going locally most of the week – and on a Thursday I would go up to Ponteland and Northumberland. It was all very hard work with unsociable hours but I was doing all I could to get back on my feet financially.

I'd moved back to Scriven House Farm but I was about to get my own place again.

Lyle's parents had left the village to move to Flaxton and Bill Pulleyn, who owned the garage in the village, had bought it. He'd put it up for rent, so I went to see him. That's how I came to move into 24 The Village, 23 May 1981, my dad's birthday.

Having got my head together, as well as now having a job again and a home for us, I rang Donna and said I'd got a house for us and to get back over here. She came back.

Our new home was a lovely, very traditional 3-bedroomed semi-detached house with a lovely big garden. Perfect. So off we go again. I'm working, humping meat, and you can work out the rest.

Donna got a part-time job on a night in an off-licence in Huntington. We had friends we had known for years and we became Vernons football pools collectors on a Friday night to earn a bit more money.

But there's something else I haven't told you. When I'd come back on my own I'd met somebody else! Diane.

Diane was a nice girl and we had a bit of fun. We weren't exactly going out together. She lived in Stillington, another nearby village, and she was a mobile hairdresser. When Donna came back Diane became her hairdresser! Oh my God!

The only thing I would say in my defence is that I'm

only 23 when this is going on, my wife and kids are over in Northern Ireland, and the marriage appears to be over. And I have needs.

But I kept seeing Diane. I'd had a taste of her and when Donna went over to Northern Ireland to see her mum with the boys during the school holidays it gave me the opportunity to see her again. I'm having an affair.

I wasn't about to leave Donna for Diane. It really was what people call 'a bit on the side' and it seemed to suit both me and Diane at the time.

I was being a plank, thinking I could have my cake and eat it. I felt in a way Donna had deserved it because she had messed me about making me go over to Northern Ireland and give up my career. I was also still only 23 and wanted to sow some wild oats again.

In May 1982 I started working for Dennis Roberts who had a pig farm in the village of Sutton on the Forest. My humping days, meat-wise, were over! On winter's days they had been horrible times. Your hands got that cold walking in and out of fridges and the bitterly cold weather. You could hardly feel your hands and had to be careful you didn't cut your finger off. You certainly wouldn't have felt it if you had.

I'd been looking for an opportunity to get back into pig farming and had seen Dennis' advertisement looking for a day-to-day manager. Dennis had built up his pig unit from nothing to 250 Large White X sows with all progeny going to bacon. His farm also included arable land growing cereals and potatoes with most of the cereals going to the pigs, who we also fed skimmed milk. Dennis was a very down-to-earth traditional farmer and I got on really well with him and his son Nigel.

Donna found out about me and Diane, of course it got out and we had a turbulent time. I think somebody else told her that her husband was seeing this other woman and when Donna confronted me I said it was true. There was absolute hell on. She was a very fiery woman. We ended up having a fight. I slapped her across the face and she hit me.

Many a time I'd go to bed on my own. Donna would then come upstairs and pull everything off the bed. Ten minutes later when I got into bed with the bedding back on Donna would do the same again. It was dreadful. In the end I moved out. Mum and Dad had a static caravan in the garden at Scriven House Farm that my mum's cousin used to stay in when they came to visit, but this was now winter time. I moved into the caravan.

Donna went back to Northern Ireland, with the children to live with her mother and the boys started their school life in Northern Ireland! My head was mashed.

Bill Pulleyn came to me and said if I wasn't living at 24 The Village he wanted the house back, even though I was still paying the rent. This might have been the catalyst for me to sort things out with Donna and we had a family discussion that involved Betty, Donna's brother Robert, Donna and me.

Robert was very ill at the time and had a kidney that had to be removed. He had to go on dialysis. Donna's gran had just died. It was never going to work for her over there and I wanted her and the boys back.

Donna came back again, with the boys, and now finally things started to settle down. I knew it was going to be hard and that she would always hold what I'd done against me. I mean, how can you have an affair when you're 23, married and have two young children, but to be fair to Donna she did try so hard to make things work and for some time it really did. I tried so hard too, but Donna would always hold the trump card as I had slept with her hairdresser and that memory was never going to go away.

We worked at our marriage and both attended marriage

guidance counselling. Looking back I can't believe we did this, but we both went into the York office and sat and talked about things. I don't think it did a lot of good to be honest, but we did try.

Around this time we got really friendly with our neighbours Peter and Daphne North. They had a son called Daniel who went to school with our boys. Tragically, Daniel went to a rave, took a drug and died. It hit us all so hard, we didn't know what to do. He was 14 years old and the apple of their eye. Our boys were devastated and it was naturally a very hard time for Peter, Daphne and all of Daniel's friends. They never got over it and sadly split up and went their different ways. His funeral was attended by hundreds and I remember watching poor Pete give a moving eulogy in tears. A sad, desperate time. I still feel for them both now.

Back to Donna and I.

Diane was still in our social group with her new boyfriend and looking back it is amazing how tolerant Donna was of her, but Diane moved away after a few years and we lost contact completely.

The boys started at Wigginton School and gradually normality came to our lives. This next period was the most stable part of what had been a tempestuous marriage up until then, some of it forced by circumstances out of our control, like Donna's father's passing. Donna was still fiery, but we did have some really good times.

Dennis paid decent money and either the first or second Christmas I worked for him he gave me £100 cash bonus. Donna and I couldn't believe it. He also gave me time off to be with Donna and the children. It was a wonderful gesture and he really was looking after us.

We liked going out and Donna always liked a drink – and a smoke. She was on Bacardi and Coke and smoked 20 cigarettes a day. Part of her family's Irish culture was that they all loved to drink. I remember her Uncle Jim, Auntie Ina and their son William, who was an usher at our wedding, were all the same. They all loved their whisky. Sadly, they had all passed during the time between her dad passing and her gran and Robert's troubles. Donna really had had it tough losing so many family members.

Our two regular pubs were The Black Horse in Wigginton and The Cottage in Haxby, where Donna worked behind the bar for quite a while before getting a job working for the Tote. She went to a number of racecourses and was on decent money. Donna was a good worker. She'd always have a part-time job. She was the best mother to our children and a superb cook. Donna looked after us all really well.

Donna was the life and soul of the party when she was on form, but in the wrong mood you really had to give her a wide berth. Her temper would often get the better of her, even on nights out with friends, and it was not unusual to see her just storm out of a house or party and go home because something did not suit. But I loved her dearly.

From the huge dramas of 1982, which also included the sad passing of my nana, who had suffered a massive aortic aneurism and died on her own in her bungalow, we had emerged into a period of largely happy family life.

Nana's passing left me inconsolable for a while that this kind-hearted, wonderful woman was no longer around. I was 24 and I don't think I'd ever cried so much in my life. I'd received a phone call from my parents to ask me to call and see them. They sat me down and told me. Uncle John had found her. I couldn't believe my father saying, 'Oh well, she was a good age.' Typical Dad, showing no emotion. I still miss her and think about her fondly and the very special relationship we shared.

Donna and I are now back working at our marriage, making it work. I'm working on a farm, with pigs, as I'd always intended. I'm on decent money for us to live okay and Donna's working too. My job involved working every other weekend, which wasn't so bad, and we had a nice home at 24 The Village where our garden at the back was so big we had three or four pet lambs running around. I had even bought a few pigs of my own that I had at Scriven House Farm. We had the odd holiday to Reighton Gap on the coast.

In 1987 Donna wasn't very well and it turned out she had cervical cancer. My poor 'honey', that was my pet name for Donna, had to have a hysterectomy and it took her a long time to recover. She was only 28, nothing of an age for a woman to have that kind of operation, so maybe having the boys when we did was all for the best even though we were so young at the time.

We wanted to buy our own home, as we were still renting 24 The Village from Bill, but I wasn't earning enough to buy one. I needed a progression from where I was with Dennis. I'd been looking after his pigs for quite a while now and had about a dozen sows of my own.

I saw an advertisement for a sales representative and AI operator working for Nitrovit, an animal feed company. It seemed the logical next step for me to utilise my knowledge of pigs and to earn more money, so that we could afford to get a home of our own. I got the job in 1987 and left Dennis, who had always been very good to me.

The job came with a nice car. The office I worked out of was in Copgrove, between Knaresborough and Boroughbridge. My role was to go out and sell pig feed to farmers and to be an artificial inseminator of pigs. Julian Norton eat your heart out! I was doing this before you!

I used to travel over to the Holderness coast in the East Riding where there were pig farms everywhere. It was vastly different to working on a farm every day and I enjoyed the experience, but it only lasted around a year.

Farming, Celebs and Plum Pudding Pigs!

There was a problem with disease somewhere or other. At the time the Porcine Reproduction & Respiratory Syndrome (PRRS) virus had been detected in USA, so it may have been that, but there have always been viruses and diseases in pigs and when they happen, they tend to go right through pig herds.

Nitrovit sacked me because I had my own pigs, but they had known I had them when I'd started. They said the only way I could stay was if I got rid of my pigs. Their justification was that I couldn't have my own pigs and then be going on to other farms. It was crazy. I was extremely safety conscious and used disinfectants and waterproofs wherever I went, always washing down my boots.

I said, 'Hang on a bit, you employed me knowing I had pigs,' but they still sacked me. I fought them over the sacking, which was another scary thing because for the first time in my life I had to use the services of a solicitor. I went with Cowling, Swift and Kitchin in York and was represented by a lady who specialised in unfair dismissal. I quite fancied her actually. I know what you're thinking. No, I didn't!

We took Nitrovit to an industrial tribunal, which was heard in court in Leeds – and we won! I won back my job, but I didn't want it by now, I had another career in mind. I just wanted to make my point – and they had to make a settlement and pay all costs.

Are you ready for Milkman Chris? Here we go!

CHAPTER 12

Confessions of Milkman Chris

I'd had this idea that I would follow dad in farming at Scriven House Farm. It's nothing new. Many farmers' sons feel the same. I'd started with some pigs at the farm and I had this field they had given me, but my dreams were shattered in 1988 when they sold the farm and moved to a lovely bungalow in Old Earswick.

I remember crying my eyes out again as I rode by, because I couldn't believe they were no longer there and that we didn't have a farm anymore. I'd been hoping to develop my little pig unit so that I could eventually earn my living from it, but that was now never going to happen. I sold my little field to the person who bought Scriven House Farm, which brought about the wherewithal to start out on my next venture after my Nitrovit experience.

It was a friend, Dave Medd, who told me that Northern Dairies on Hull Road in York were advertising one of their franchised milk rounds in the city.

Dave and his wife Barbara, or 'Barberra' as she is sometimes called affectionately in the way Tom Courtenay said the name in *The Royle Family* TV show, were friends and have become very close to me. Respect goes to them as they have known me and my three wives intimately, which must have proved quite difficult for them at times over the years!

Dave had been with Northern all his life and was a supervisor. He told me it could offer a good income and as I was motivated to buy a house and find something that was our own for Donna, myself and the boys, rather than renting, I applied.

Northern Dairies wanted their franchisees to present the company in the right way and I had to go away on a training course to become a milkman. I think I went to Wakefield. You soon understand why a course is needed because there's much more to being a milkman than simply picking up the empties and delivering that day's orders. It is a business and you are responsible for it. You collect the money, you pick up your milk at a certain time of day, you drive a milk float, you wear a uniform, you build up your customer base. You are running your own little business within theirs.

They helped show how you should run it. Straight away I saw the incentive. The more people I could get, the more I could earn. It offered the opportunity of earning around £500 a week which, in 1988, was good money to me and probably double what I'd been earning up to that point.

There's an initial down payment you have to make, and that's where the income from selling my field at Scriven House Farm came in. Firstly, you paid Northern Dairies a £3000 deposit for the round. It's your commitment to them; after all, you're using their milk float and delivering their produce. The deposit was returned when you finished with your franchise.

People don't always understand this next bit but you also buy what is called the 'debt on the book'. What this means is that when you take over there is always a certain amount of money outstanding from customers, no matter how many times the previous milkman has called to receive the monies. It's probably different today if milkmen are set up with card machines or those who have doorstep delivery may also pay by BACS, but in my day it was largely cash and cheques. So, I managed to cover the costs of the deposit and the book and I got started.

My milk round was Woodthorpe, a suburb to the south west of York, delivering 100 gallons of milk every day, 6 days a week. These were the days when doorstep delivery of milk was much bigger than it is today. The supermarkets hadn't yet started taking over and glass bottles were still the king.

I used to start at 1 o'clock in the morning, picking up my round from Hull Road, and I was home for 8 o'clock. All of a sudden I've got time at home in the daytime. I'd go to bed at 1 in the afternoon and sleep until about 6-7 o'clock, so I could then be with the kids and Donna for a bit. Then I'd go to bed again for a couple of hours and get up at midnight for the milk round. It was a crazy life, but it was good money as Dave had said it would be.

I did really well at this and increased the round quite a lot just by putting in the hard work and going right around my round adding to it. For every gallon I increased my milk round Northern Dairies would give me £100, so I quite quickly managed to increase it by another 10 gallons a day and received a £1000 bonus.

Having a proper income and now a good income enabled us to get a mortgage and in July 1989 we bought a 3-bedroomed semi-detached home in Usher Lane in Haxby. I was back on my feet. Family, job, house, a nice car – this time a Vauxhall Cavalier Sport, a big bright red family car, quite sporty looking – and a bit of money in the bank.

Our first foreign holiday as a family was in 1990 and it all came about through Robert, Donna's brother. He'd told us all we needed was to buy flights to Mallorca and he would meet us at the airport where he would take us to this villa he had rented with its own pool.

The villa was amazing and we had a fantastic week with Robert and his friend Jim, and Donna's mum Betty. They had thought we needed a bit of a break and it turned out a super holiday for which I shall be forever grateful.

The milk round was good money, but the problem was the hours. It wasn't just the delivering, it was also the collecting of the money, that was Thursday night or sometimes also Friday night and Saturday morning, just to make sure you were keeping on top of the debt. I was regularly doing 60 hours a week minimum. It was quite stressful at times, but I was fit. The one night I could go out was a Saturday, because I could have a lie-in on a Sunday morning.

I was a milkman for nearly five years from July 1988 to May 1993 and although we now had our own house and car and had other foreign holidays the pressure of the hours I was putting in started taking its toll. I wanted to be out of being a milkman, but the problem was the money was so good. At the end of 1992 I gave up my franchised round, but I continued to deliver for Northern Dairies on different rounds and became contracted on other areas in New Earswick and Elvington. I'd had enough really and was marking time until I found another job that might pay as well as the milk.

Donna always loved to party and we both enjoyed our social life, but the milk round took over and she ended up going out with friends on her own, clubbing. I remember one night I was waiting to go out on my round, I usually left home around half past midnight, and Donna hadn't come home. I was annoyed that she didn't get home until around 1 o'clock and that's when the cracks started to reappear in our relationship. We were going downhill again at this point.

There were one or two instances where my job as a milkman saw me get rather close to one or two women and with one of them, well, we did it on the milk float!

One summer's morning I was delivering milk to a house when the door opened and this woman was stood there almost completely naked. She opened whatever she had on to show me everything, grabbed me and my God she was red hot! Her name was Melanie, I think, we'd chatted on the doorstep previously when I'd collected money and I was always flirty. She'd clearly stayed up for me to call and I think her husband was only upstairs. We had a quick grope. I just couldn't believe it. I certainly had a smile on my face the rest of that day!

The girl on the milk float was quite another story! She was called Val and had massive tits. She lived in a council house on my round and was helping me with the round at four in the morning one summer's day. It was quite a warm start to the day and her birthday. We'd stopped at the end of a street for a quick cup of coffee. She gave me a kiss and that just led from one thing to another – right there, right then – on the float. She didn't have a bra on, I remember that much, and it was like wow! Incredible! It happened a few times more!

And here's another story! Val got pregnant! I never saw her again. I'd gone round to her house to see her about giving her more work, so I still don't know to this day what happened. Maybe there's another little Farmer Chris running around somewhere? He or she, if ever born, would be in his or her early twenties now.

CHAPTER 13

Pearl Assurance – and the end of me and Donna – and nearly the end of my life!

I can't believe that I did it now, but I became a Pearl Assurance representative. You know the ones that used to come out and sell you a life assurance policy or pension? That was me from May 1993 to 1994.

These were the months that broke me, nearly killed me and eventually saw me start to once again rebuild my life – without Donna.

One of my milk delivery customers was a manager for Pearl and I had been talking to him about giving up my job with Northern Dairies. He'd mentioned about 'taking a book out' with Pearl. I asked what he meant by the phrase and he said you were given a 'book' for an area where weekly or monthly payments were due on the policies, as was the Pearl way, and you collected them in each week. It seemed a bit like collecting the money owed for the milk, so since I was used to that I thought I'd give it a go.

It was a little bit more than collecting money. The regional office was based in Northallerton and they trained you about the legislative stuff.

I've got to tell you it was all wrong. There was a lot going on about pensions and life assurance in the press at the time and we were still selling policies and making good money from doing so. We didn't really care about you, the customer. It was all about the commission we could earn – and that's how we were taught! It was really bad. You could go and sell a life assurance policy or pension and you could earn £500 in one night, but people were sold the wrong products.

It was another odd job once again because of the hours. It was night work mainly as most people back then were at work during the day. I would be out on the prowl for Pearl business from 6 o'clock while 10 o'clock at night. Again, it wasn't the best of hours to allow for going out together but Donna and I used to go out quite a bit to what was called the Caravan Club at Rawcliffe on the A19.

Just the week before Christmas in December 1993 my world collapsed. We were at the club having what I felt had been a good time. We always spoke to others, flirted, had a few drinks, both of us.

'I'm not coming home with you,' were the words Donna said and off she went with this man from the club. I was stunned, devastated, shocked – none of those words are good enough, but put them all together and add a few more like being hit by a sledgehammer or distraught and you'll have an idea how I felt at that moment.

I didn't know what to do, how to react, what I should say. Stuart (Smallwood) and his wife Barbara took me back home to Haxby that night. My head was spinning. It had come totally out of the blue.

Some reading this will probably think I was getting all I deserved. Karma is what some will feel. This had now happened to me. My wife has gone off with another man, to his house. Some will no doubt say that at least she told me what she was doing.

I then started going through the strangest time ever.

Donna came home the following day. We had massive words. Christmas was around the corner. She didn't go back to him. All I wanted was her to be back for good. I couldn't believe she'd want to go off with another man. I was shocked, uncertain and terrified I was going to lose her.

Farming, Celebs and Plum Pudding Pigs!

I've never really been able to work myself out. To this day I can see another woman and think I would love to go to bed with you, and in my younger life I did and to hell with the consequences.

It's really very strange because I did love Donna, really loved her and not in the same way as I did then, but I still love her now and I'm sure she still has a love for me. I just don't understand my lust for other women when I had a lovely wife. Why did I put all of that in jeopardy by playing around? I'm shaking my head as I write this, just so you know.

I think Donna may have done it before with this man. I don't think that night when she said she wasn't coming home with me was the first time, now that I think about the lead up to that night. The nights I was collecting my money as a Pearl Assurance guy or maybe further back as a milkman. I believe there were others too, but whether there were or there weren't it is of no odds now and I'd never hold any of it against her. I think that's something that happened because she realised I was doing it.

Our relationship was coming to its end, which was a bloody shame. We had a lot to look forward to and we'd both worked hard. We had a lovely home and lovely children. Going back, having married so young put us under pressure for many years, but somehow we had managed around 16 years as man and wife before it all came crashing down.

And boy did my life take a strange turn of events into the early part of 1994. We had got through Christmas and New Year. Donna and I were laid together and starting to make love when she got up and said, 'I just can't do this anymore.' Off she went, back to 'him' in Rawcliffe. She came back again the following day, but then I decided to go and stay with Mum and Dad, leaving Donna at home with the boys.

Next thing I know 'he' has moved in! He's moved in to our house in Haxby. He's now living in my marital home! And he's in our marital bed with my wife!

I'm puddled mentally by this. I told you things were strange around now, and they got stranger still. I'm up at Mum and Dad's and I'm still working for Pearl. I then do something very stupid.

I took some money. It was £50. It was hardly robbing the Bank of England. I'd taken £50 from the money I was collecting because I was short of cash, instead of banking it as I was meant to. I then wrote a cheque that bounced. Pearl sacked me for falsifying accounts. I paid the money back. I'd only needed it for convenience, for a night out, it was the daftest of things.

I just didn't give a fuck about anything anymore. I just felt terrible thinking about my wife, my children, this other man in my house. What the hell have I done?

Robert, Donna's brother, rang me from Northern Ireland and in his thick Irish accent said, 'Christopher! What are you doing? What ARE you doing?' He was really forceful. 'You get yourself back into that house! You ring them tonight and you tell them that you are moving back on Monday morning and whether they are there or not, you move back in.'

I was close to Robert and I did as he said. I rang Donna and told her I would be back on Monday. I remember I'd gone round to the house on Valentine's Day with a red rose and had said to Donna, 'I still love you,' and she'd basically said, 'Fuck off.'

This time, when I went back home, it was different.

She wasn't there for one thing, and neither was he. I drove into the driveway and set foot back in my home once again. They'd taken the dishwasher and the dog, a Pekinese called Ming Ming, and all Donna's clothes.

They totally messed with my mind though, when I

entered the bedroom, what had been our bedroom. There were grapes all over the bed! It was as though they were saying they'd had a lovely time. It has stuck with me all those years and will never leave.

I was back home, but this was a very difficult period. I sat down and talked with the boys who were now 15 and 14. I just said, 'It's just me and you now.'

In the first month or two Donna would occasionally come back to make sure the boys were okay, but after that time they didn't see her for at least two years.

This is the only time in my life I have felt suicidal.

That's when, on a dark, dank February morning in 1994 I was feeling at the lowest point in my life ever. I'd lost Donna, lost my job, had by now negative equity in our house, was struggling to pay the mortgage and was feeling well and truly sorry for myself, but worse still blaming myself for everything. If I hadn't had that affair with Diane it would have been so different, wouldn't it?

It was all getting too much as I looked out of our house that day. I was wrecked. There seemed only one possible solution.

That's when I remembered what Dad had said about the fastest stretch of track between Darlington and York on the railway line. I wouldn't be the first to give up my life there.

That's when I took my bicycle out and pedalled in the direction of Overton to the grass paddock where Dad used to take me and my brothers on a Sunday morning.

Almost immediately a train thundered by. I took my place on the line. It wouldn't be long. The trains run quite often. It's a busy line.

That's when I had this image of Dad smiling and smoking his pipe in the paddock with my brothers and Mum.

That's when I came to my senses. I thought, 'Why are

you doing this?' and told myself, 'You bloody idiot,' or as they say in Ireland, 'Catch yourself on.'

My children stopped me. They weren't there physically, but things suddenly crystalised in my mind. My boys. I'd brought them here as my dad had done with me and my brothers. This is an area of pleasure, not pain.

I cycled home. It was cold and wet, but I had found out something about myself. Yes, I was low, very low, but I had to carry on, not just for my children but for me and my family too. When I got home I put the radio on. D:ream's big hit 'Things Can Only Get Better' was playing. It became my inspiration. I still wasn't right by any means, but I'd started to realise this wasn't the end. It had to be a new beginning. I owed my kids big time. Yes, I'd cocked up my marriage and was still in love with my wife who had left me, but now I had to go forward.

I'd never understood about mental illness before and still struggle now when people say they are mentally ill, but I was mentally ill back then and realised I needed help.

CHAPTER 14

Back to College, Back with Diane and Back in Business

'I'm not well, Mum, I've got to see somebody.' That's how I put it to Mum when I went to see her that day as I attempted to get my life back on track. Being a nurse, Mum had some good contacts and she had a friend who was a therapist who lived in York and saw me out of her normal hours at her home as a favour to Mum.

This lady helped me get my head right. She got me to write down what I was thinking and why I was thinking it. What came out of our sessions most of all was that I had two lovely boys, who I'm so proud of every day of my life; and that while I accepted I'd been no saint, part of me felt physically and mentally rejected by my wife.

The first thing I had to do was to look after the boys and myself – and to do that I needed some form of income. I still had a mortgage to pay and this was the time when mortgage rates had rocketed to 15% after we'd bought the house in Haxby. I was unemployed since I'd lost my job at Pearl.

I went on 'the social' where they assess your full situation and ended up getting quite a good amount of money, but I could only claim for half the mortgage payment with Donna expected to pay the other half. The only problem with that was she didn't, and I could see it from her point of view. She wasn't living there, so why should she? I then received a letter telling me my house was to be repossessed because I wasn't paying the whole mortgage.

I ended up going to the magistrates' court to plead my case and the magistrate let me keep the house and ordered that the outstanding debt be added to the loan. Payments could be made by me via money from the social to bring it up to date.

Our divorce came through quite quickly. Donna had gone and was hoping to marry her man.

My mate Rob (Dent) and Richard (Newby) looked after me with work at this time. Rob has a farm and I started working a bit for him, initially lambing sheep in spring 1994. He was paying me cash, which was helping, and I was learning very quickly how to cook, wash, iron and clean the house.

Richard could see I was struggling and gave me some part-time work looking after his pigs. I really appreciated all that both Rob and Richard did for me.

The Newbys are a lovely family. Sadly, Richard's parents Ernest and Elsie have now passed. Richard and his lovely wife Fran who farm at Plainville Farm, Wigginton, have two lovely daughters Claire and Gemma. They have a really good farming business run with his brother George.

Back to me. In the kitchen.

I'd never cooked before and it wasn't the fanciest food ever, but I could do a decent joint of meat, some very basic mashed potato and Yorkshire pudding.

I've never got my head around why an ironing board is shaped that way. Not everything I ironed was a success as David will tell you. I completely trashed his favourite baseball top, but he and his brother Rob were very understanding. They knew I was trying my best.

Being born in September and the following August the boys were in the same school year and were at Joseph Rowntree School in New Earswick. They both enjoyed their football. Rob was a striker and David a midfielder.

Farming, Celebs and Plum Pudding Pigs!

They played for Wigginton Grasshoppers FC that my Uncle John set up in 1980. We became even closer, as it was just the three of us and even went into Minster FM and had our own divorce party on air!

Financially I was still in a mess. It wasn't just the mortgage. When Donna and I split we had nothing but debt and negative equity of around £15,000. Life had always been a constant battle to keep our heads above water.

It was now that I thought I had to do something with my life. This is really the start of how Farmer Chris ended up coming about. If I hadn't taken this next step, I certainly wouldn't have taken all the other steps that have followed on more naturally – even though with a few Randy Chris moments along the way! Stay tuned!

I decided I was going to go back to college as a mature student. Farming is in my blood, in my veins and I wanted to get back into it in some way. Pearl Assurance for goodness' sake? How had I let that happen? It was time to focus.

Rob and Richard had been great, but I knew for them it was about helping me out and for me the work was just that, it was helping me financially and getting my head sorted.

But I knew that dipping ewes and lambing sheep wasn't the way I wanted the rest of my life to go. Even when I started back at college, Rob still gave me part-time work and Rob knows how much that meant to me. He, Stuart and Lyle have always been there for me, so boys, take a bow here.

College had changed completely since my first time around in the 70s. Back then you were in all day, five days a week, apart from the Wednesday afternoon sports. This time you had a lot of free time and that suited me wonderfully well because I'm a single parent, I need to earn money and I'm retraining for a career in the future that I didn't know about yet. All I wanted at the time was to get a new qualification, earn some additional money and look after the boys.

I'd taken on a 2-year course for an HND in Agriculture at Askham Bryan College and ended up taking the option to top it up to three years and get my degree, which I completed in May 1997. I came out with a BSc Honours degree in Agriculture and one of the highlights of my life was going to Leeds University in gown and cap and throwing my cap into the air, proud as punch at 39 years of age.

I had a wonderful time as a mature student and the younger ones used to take the mickey out of me as 'the old boy'. I continued working hard with Rob and for other people, getting jobs where I could and although it was still tough financially, I managed to buy a really cheap Ford Fiesta Mk 1. I finally felt I was going somewhere and had a focus (no, it really was a Fiesta! Ha ha).

During my second run of college years there was another very important person who came back into my life!

I'd been on my own for around a year when Diane and I got back together at the beginning of 1995. But, typically of me, it was a bit messy. She was married. Uh-oh! Here we go again!

I'd got it into my head, wondering what she was doing now. I made enquiries and discovered through a friend of mine that she was unhappily married. We got in touch and she came to see me. She was clearly unhappy, and I was on my own. She told me her husband controlled her and that she was afraid of him.

Diane was a very homely, loving, caring and practical woman and realizing I was doing everything on my own she would often call in with a meal she had prepared for me and the boys. She didn't stay to eat, but gradually she started helping with the other domestic duties. She then split with her husband and was now living with her parents in Stillington. We started seeing a bit more of each other. We didn't go out as a couple as such, but we were getting closer and it wasn't so long before she stayed over. I guess part of me was looking for someone to share my life with and so that we had a family again, and someone who could help with the home and the children.

Something quite serious then happened. This was quite a dramatic and scary time as her husband was a violent man who had a bit of a history with firearms! And he had a shotgun licence! Oh my God, once again! How do I pick 'em!

One morning, after Diane had stayed over, we set off in my car to take her to work. We drove out of the drive and into the street in Haxby. Diane looked up and said, 'Oh, fucking hell, just drive to Fulford police station, now!'

He'd got wind that she'd been staying with me, had found out where I lived and had parked down the road stalking us. When we set off, he followed. She said, 'He will shoot you.' Jesus Christ! Thanks for the reassurance!

I drove straight to the police station and when they eventually stopped him he was arrested for using threatening behaviour. He had a 12-bore in his car, so Diane wasn't exactly way off the mark with her prediction. He was a very nasty, dangerous man and threatened me on the phone several times in the coming weeks and months.

We married at Haxby Methodist Church in October 1995, while I was in the second year of my HND course at Askham Bryan, after nearly a year of seeing each other. It seemed the sensible thing to do at the time, but even then her now ex-husband reappeared by phoning me at home on the day of the wedding with a very sinister message almost threatening to be at the wedding to disrupt the day. He didn't.

When I think back now Diane fitted. She was so good at doing everything at home that myself and the boys never wanted for anything. The house was spotless. We ate fantastic home-cooked food, she had a nice car, she brought another income to the home having changed her job from mobile hairdresser to a professional cook, she had become head chef at Askham Bryan College, where I was studying, which is where we had been going when her husband followed us that day.

Things were getting better, and we had holidays abroad. I know this next bit is terrible but Diane was providing me with everything I needed at the time after Donna – food, cleaning and sex. Yes, I know that's terrible but I'm telling it like it was.

The wedding was done on the rebound and in hindsight it was a massive mistake. As you get older you hope to become wiser and you can look back on things. The boys didn't like her, and they never got on, no matter how much Diane tried and she really did try her best. It wasn't a great situation, but in some ways it wasn't bad either. We had a nice little life going. I had a bit of stability and we muddled through. We enjoyed our honeymoon in Ibiza and holidays in Mallorca, but there was never the spark there. I was never actually in love with Diane and I think she knew that deep down we should never have married.

Donna had married her man that September, just the month before our wedding and I'd thought, 'I'll show you.' I'd imagined Donna's marriage wouldn't last 6 months. They're still together today! And I am very happy for them both. His name's Martin. He's a nice bloke.

The boys tolerated Diane for me. I only found that out from them later in life, and that they had both left home to get their own houses inspired by a will to get away from their wicked stepmother! Diane was never ever wicked.

We had been able to have Donna's name removed from the title deeds and mortgage to 25 Usher Lane in Haxby and Diane's included instead. It became our marital home and we spent a lot of time and money on improving it before eventually selling for a slight profit. Property prices had started to improve, which meant we were out of negative equity and we paid off the mortgage arrears.

I fitted a bath, a toilet, a sink, all the pipes; I boarded out the loft where we made a room for Robert; I even hired a scaffolding tower to knock a hole in the gable end to fit a window! None of it would have got past any kind of regulations and the planks on my scaffolding were already dodgy before I put a coffee table on them so that I could reach to knock bricks out. I didn't have a clue what I was doing really but I was just trying to make the home better.

Early in 1996 Donna and I had been back in touch. It had been two years since any of us had seen her and she started coming to the boys' sports events and school meetings. It also got to the point where the boys were going over to Northern Ireland with Donna and Martin. That hurt me a bit, but I remember one funny moment the first time they went as they hadn't wanted to leave me behind. They rang me from their bedroom. I really didn't like the idea of them getting on well with Martin, but bridges were being built between Donna and the boys and that was the right thing.

They whispered to me on the phone, 'Dad, are you alright? We're not meant to be ringing you.' It was very thoughtful of them.

Donna and I don't keep in touch now, but we have each other's mobile numbers should anything occur with the boys. She lives in a village not far from Kate and I, with Martin. They have a garden shop where they sell her homemade baking and preserves. She was always good at that.

As my degree course was nearing its end in May 1997 I saw an advertisement that was to steer me on to the business path that eventually saw me able to fulfil my lifetime's ambition and become Farmer Chris, not the TV show person, but the farmer I always wanted to be right at the start.

I was in the library at Leeds University and saw an advertisement for an animal health salesperson for Laycock's agricultural chemists at their tiny little bothy in Malton. Their main base was in Skipton and they were a reputable company looking to spread their wings in the eastern side of Yorkshire.

My first thought was wow, this sounds good and it was just the kind of thing I'd been training for, something in the agricultural world and in the retail world where I could make my mark and earn good money. I rang the owner Jeff Marsden who was an agricultural pharmacist and he offered me the job. He thought it was wonderful that I had an agricultural degree. He'd never had anybody work for him previously who'd had one.

I said goodbye to being on benefits and dipping sheep for cash and started in June 1997. My own boss. I loved it. I had a van and a salary plus commission. Right from the start I saw Laycock's as a sleeping giant. I'm a natural salesperson and with my combined previous experience of selling either milk or pensions and my agricultural background I knew I could take this somewhere. I had sales increasing every month with an expanding portfolio of stock and within a very short period of time the little Malton branch was turning over £200,000 a year!

I told Jeff we needed to move to bigger premises where we could do so much more and within a year we had moved to new premises, quadrupling the size of our unit, on Showfield Lane Industrial Estate in Malton.

CHAPTER 15

Robert and Robert – A Tale of Two Robs

There have been three Roberts who have all played major roles in my life – first, there's my son; second, there's Rob Dent part of our Fab 4 including Stuart and Lyle; and third there's Robert, Donna's brother. This next tale came about in 1996, while I was at Askham Bryan College, second time around.

Bless Donna's family, they'd had some bad luck healthwise, and her brother Robert who was now in his 40s had not been well. He'd lost one kidney and the other that was left was the size of a pea. A suitable donor was required, Donna wasn't suitable and at the time there were questions about Robert and David, being relatives. I spent a lot of time with Robert in Northern Ireland and we got on, but I was petrified of the consequences if my Rob or David donated their kidney.

Around the same time as Robert was nearing his end over in Northern Ireland my mum said, 'There's something wrong with this boy. He's losing a lot of weight.' I thought maybe it had to do with the breakup of me and Donna. It had obviously been a hard and stressful time for all of us and I'd thought the boys had taken it very well, but maybe I hadn't realised that Rob hadn't taken it as well as I'd thought.

Mum had noticed because, ever since Donna had left and then Diane had come back on my scene, he was spending a lot of time with my mum and dad at Old Earswick.

Rob was working as a coalman at the time and was a

big, strong, strapping six-foot, 17-year-old. We took him to the doctor who immediately referred him for tests.

Mum was straight on it: 'We're going to pay for him to go to a Nuffield hospital,' and that's where they diagnosed that he had Crohn's disease. Oddly enough Diane had it as well. Rob's case was quite severe and it was a really worrying time, but within a month he was in and had surgery. They had to remove a significant quantity of his intestine. It was a big operation and he was in hospital a couple of weeks.

While Rob was in hospital his Irish uncle Robert passed away. David and I decided we would have to go and tell his brother that his uncle had died. Remember, Rob had just had a big operation himself. It was all serious stuff.

So, David and I go into the hospital and we thought about how we were going to break it to him that his uncle had passed away. Rob thought a lot of Robert, as we all did, and Rob had known he was ill, but wouldn't have expected him to die. We just thought we couldn't wait until Rob came out of hospital so we asked the nurse whether we could go into a private room with him, as we had something we needed to talk about.

Rob was on a drip on the ward and was still not back to normal since his operation. I said, 'Rob, we've something to tell you. We need to go somewhere quiet, in another room. He said, 'Okay.' I remember he wasn't yet walking very well after his operation and he was pushing along his mobile drip.

When we got into the room Rob just looked at us and said, 'Am I going to die?' We hadn't thought this through, had we? It's obvious now that we should have realised how what we were saying and the action of going somewhere quieter could be misconstrued, particularly after his operation, but we didn't, we just looked at each other and

I then said, 'No Rob, you're not. It's your uncle Robert.'

Hindsight is such a wonderful thing and maybe we should have just said, 'We've something to tell you, but don't worry, it's not about you.'

Funnily enough I spoke with Rob about that incident recently and Rob said, 'Dad, I'll never ever forget that conversation.'

CHAPTER 16

Going Green

I met Kate on my first day at Laycock's in May 1997, but not for long as she had her own sheep and was heading off to Nottinghamshire County Show at Newark, the show before the Yorkshire summer show season kicks off with Otley Show, the oldest agricultural show in the country, the week later.

Kate was working part-time for Jeff (Marsden) and had been for a few years, she had been working alongside a girl called Judy Hickes who also worked part-time, but Judy was pregnant and was due to leave later that year. Rather than replace her with another part-time person Jeff had decided to bite the bullet and take things forward at Malton with someone full-time – and that was me.

So, Kate and I met and off she went to the show. I was left for the rest of the day with a representative from one of the companies we bought from.

Little did either Kate or I know what our coming together at Malton would lead to in the subsequent 20-plus years! In that time we've built our own business, become husband and wife, shared so much together and are now both back to our first love – the countryside and farming.

But let's not get all misty eyed about cattle, sheep, pigs, horses and dogs just yet. This is me remember, and things have a habit of taking several twists and turns – and we were just 'the new boy' and 'the young lady going off to a show' that day.

I worked for Jeff for seven years and had some really

good times going on courses, being wined and dined by suppliers, and building the business for him.

The lion's share of Jeff's business, as the Laycock's agricultural chemists name suggests, when I started was most definitely animal medicines and chemists' products. The one major advantage Jeff had was that he was a chemist and could dispense medicines to farmers, and all his team had to have the AMTRA (Animal Medicines Training Regulatory Authority) certificate in order to advise and sell prescription medicines for livestock to farmers.

Kate and Judy already had their qualifications so one of my first missions was to go back to college!

To gain my AMTRA qualification I was to attend a one-week residential course at Harper Adams University at Edgmond near Newport in Shropshire. There were around 20 of us from all over the country and we had a ball!

I mean, we were all thirty somethings, staying in college digs and it was literally study, eat, study, drink, shag, repeat! Well, okay, not everyone you understand, but I somehow got involved with these two Scottish girls and they were, well, quite warm!

What is a red-blooded male to do when he is put into pairs to study during the evening, in our bloody bedrooms? One of them was my age and from Wick and she really liked, errm! Well, you know, and as I recall she loved sexy lingerie too! The other was from Stirling and only 28 and my goodness she was making the most of her stay as was I! We had a fabulous time acting like teenagers and yes, we did qualify when we went back for a second week for the exams.

I had two wonderful trips to Ireland through the Irish dairy co-operative Dairygold in the Golden Vale area of Co Cork. They are one of the largest dairy co-operatives in Ireland and one of the biggest manufacturers of milk powders.

On one of the trips we were taken to Bunratty Castle in Co Clare. It is a 15th century tower house between Limerick and Ennis. In the evening we were in this pub called Dirty Nellie's. There were about 20 of us who had been invited from England and there were what seemed 100s inside, but this guy came up to me and said, quite demonstratively, 'YOU! You have been messing with these buxom serving wenches!'

For once in my life I was absolutely in the clear! I knew I hadn't done anything. I was just on a jolly with Dairygold. I started to resist. I hadn't done anything wrong.

It was all a set-up. The guy who had taken us to the pub had made me the fall guy! I was the one to be picked on.

The long and short of this was I had to go and sing on stage for my supper. I always wanted to be able to sing. The problem is I'm tone deaf! It would have been easier for me to speak Martian than sing. They threw me into the cells at the back of the stage and I had to rattle the bars and shout 'let me out!'. Eventually the audience, the rest of the pub, were cajoled into letting me out on the condition I at least tried to sing.

The only song I could come up with was the Yorkshire anthem 'On Ilkley Moor Bar Tat'. To those who don't know what it means, it is dialect for 'without a hat'. I started. They were dumbfounded but started clapping. It was awful, of course, but it was all good-natured.

One of my biggest achievements came after just two years at Laycock's when I was shortlisted for an award in the Agricultural Trade Awards for animal health sales in the country. The final part of my entry was to prepare a presentation to a board of judges, all respected professionals. I sought the help of my former mentor and ex-Askham Bryan College lecturer Bernard Ashworth.

The final was held at the Birmingham Metropole Hotel and was followed by a gala black tie dinner and award ceremony hosted by Bob Monkhouse. To say I was nervous was an understatement. I was bricking it. Winning would mean national recognition from my contemporaries, great PR and the small matter of a 5-star holiday to Mauritius for 2 weeks all inclusive!

It was like a scene from TV's *The Apprentice* when all the contestants are sat in Lord Sugar's office waiting to be called into the boardroom. When my turn of the five came, I was third in. 'Come on CJ,' as I was known then, 'you can do it,' is what I told myself.

I came out thinking I'd blown it. I am always very critical of myself and although I knew I'd given it my best shot, as I always do, and had spoken from the heart, I just had a feeling it hadn't been enough. But I could do no more.

Diane, Kate and Jeff arrived together for the evening where there were to be many awards. The room looked absolutely amazing. Two huge screens, one on each side of the stage. This was a proper awards evening with 300 people. After the wonderful dinner, music and fabulous entertainment from Bob Monkhouse, who was very funny, it was time for the awards with Bob as compere.

When my name came up on the screen as one of the finalists, in front of all these people, my heart was about to explode out of my chest.

Then came the announcement: 'And the winner is ...' My heart was pounding even more. '... Chris Jeffery of Laycock's Agricultural Chemists.'

Christ! I couldn't believe it. Everyone was kissing me, shaking my hand, but then a spotlight was on me and suddenly there I was on the screens! I received my award from Bob. I was so proud. I'd done it! And the huge bonus was that I was also going on an all expenses paid holiday to Mauritius!

My good friend Jonathan Reay deserves a mention here. He represented the company (Zoetis) that sponsored my award. 'Jonners' was the first representative I met when I joined Laycock's. He is very much like me and exactly the same age, but obviously not as good looking! He was with us all at this fabulous night when I won the prize and has become a very good friend. He is still in the business now working for Chanelle.

I don't remember much about the rest of the night as it involved copious amounts of beer and wine and champagne! The next morning I woke up with the trophy alongside me and Diane in bed.

My favourite customer while at Laycock's, because he was so full of fun, was Rob Mackley. What a guy! He's a real rough 'n' ready, bearded, indestructible, entertaining country farmer from Stape in the North York Moors, which is pretty much in the middle of nowhere except to other people in Stape!

I'd been riding around in my truck for a few days with people blowing their horns at me, waving and flashing their headlights and I'd kind of wondered why it was happening a bit more than the odd occasion – then one morning, as I was washing the truck, I got to the front. Rob had made a dummy plate with SEXY1 and had fastened it to my truck!

Farmers sometimes have a funny way of telling you things, as though it's a bit of a game rather than telling you straight away. It's a way of the countryside, I guess.

Rob was a master of the art! He rang me one day and said, 'I want some compensation!'

You see what I mean? Putting you on the wrong foot immediately. He followed up with, 'My prize goose is dead.' That's when I knew it was a wind-up, very rarely in life do you hear of anyone having a prize goose, but also I knew he wouldn't have rung without a degree of truth. Now I just had to find out what he was driving at.

'What do you mean, Mackley?' I said with similar exasperation combined with a tinge of humour.

'Your van!' he said. 'Up in my woods! Moving from side to side. I followed them. There's two of them in there having a bit of nookie, then all of a sudden the evidence gets thrown out of the bloody van. And my goose is there, swallowed it and he's dead!'

They're very good these farmers, playing it straight yet you know they're having a laugh while making their point. I said, 'What the hell are you on about Mackley?'

'My goose swallowed a condom!'

This was Rob's way of telling me that my van or rather a van with Laycock's on the side of the van, driven by a rep we had taken on, was parked on his land and he was up in this wood, shagging. It was nothing to do with a goose.

Worse still this was in 2001. Foot and Mouth epidemic year when there were restrictions on going on to farms and we couldn't travel anywhere.

The following week I'm in a meeting in Malton and our rep comes to the door asking if we, Laycock's, are insured for a member of staff getting beaten up!

He said, 'Look at my legs.' They were red raw. It turned out the husband of the woman he'd been with had beaten him up and he was trying to get Laycock's to look after him! Little did he know what I knew, thanks to Rob Mackley!

Rob is an amazing guy and quite wild. He fell off the Hole of Horcum, quite a drop, on a bike. He was on a ledge, smashed to bits and the Air Ambulance came. It wasn't enough, they had to bring a Sea King. You or I, whoever you are now reading this, would have been dead, but a bit like the TV show *The Six Million Dollar Man* from the 70s they rebuilt him, screwed him back together and after six months in hospital he emerged. Remarkable man, great sense of humour. I had a lot of time for him.

I'd been going along quite nicely at Laycock's until about the last year in 2004. By that time, I was getting frustrated with Jeff. I was doing well for him and when we parted, I'd turned it into three-quarters of a million turnover. In return all I wanted was a bit more money and a Daihatsu Fourtrak. I'm not sure to this day why I particularly wanted that, but I knew I wanted a 4WD truck and that would do. He bought me a basic model. I was happy with getting it, but still fed up.

I'd talked with Kate about finding premises elsewhere and setting up on my own – and if I did, I wanted her to come with me. We made a good team. I said, 'You are part of what we have done here.' Kate's never been ambitious in that way, but I knew she would come with me if I could find the right kind of thing.

Lo and behold in February 2004 something came up that was to lead to everything else that has happened since.

Guy Swindlehurst has been in the industry since I joined Laycock's and has become a very good friend along with his wife Jules. We have been to many social events together and he is still in the business with Elanco. It is Guy to whom I owe a great debt because if he hadn't given me some news, well I don't think there would have been a Farmer Chris. So, Guy take a bow here.

Guy had known I was looking for something, wanting to go on my own, or at least on my own but with Kate, and it was he who told me that Ray Green had died.

My first comment was, 'Who the hell's Ray Green?' In the farming world you tend to know people in your immediate radius from where you either farm or trade but not much further.

Farming, Celebs and Plum Pudding Pigs!

Ray had run his own livestock medicine and feed supplies business from a little bothy at Northallerton livestock market in Applegarth for 20 years or more. Guy told me I needed to get over there pronto and gave me Jackie's contact details, Ray's wife.

We arranged to go and see Jackie and her adviser because although it was a difficult time for her, she knew that she didn't want to take it on herself and wanted to let it go. Kate and I met Jackie at her home near Northallerton.

We told Jackie and this chap all about us, what we had been doing and what we wanted to do. I thought they had taken to us, but this guy then said, 'Tomorrow night, Farmway will be sat where you are to put their case.' My heart sank. Farmway was a big company, way bigger than Laycock's and we were trying to start on our own from Jeff. What chance had we against them in taking over Ray's business? We were way out of our depth if they were involved.

But I had been to my bank, HSBC in Malton, and Kate had been to hers, putting in our business plan. We both put in for equal monies, received the agreement before we went and were able to make our offer for the business, to operate as Ray Green Animal Health. We told Jackie it was all we could afford.

24 hours later we received a call from Jackie who said, 'Congratulations! You've got it!' Kate and I were over the moon. When we spoke later to finalise the deal Jackie said, 'I always wanted Ray's business to go to people, rather than a company.' We had just been ourselves, we just had our personalities and that's what Jackie saw. I'm really proud of that.

Kate was married, and so was I. We weren't romantically involved with each other. It was business and friendship. She's a farmer's daughter, Kate Dickinson. Her family's farm is at Brompton by Sawdon where her brother farms today. She married a farm worker David Williamson, but she wasn't happily married. They lived in a bungalow her father had bought for her.

The crazy thing that was going on at the same time as Kate and I were attempting to buy Ray's business was that Farmway were advertising a really good job offering a bigger salary than I was on with Jeff, a nice car and a good holiday package. I got an interview where I met the directors at The Black Swan in Helmsley. We'd already been to see Jackie and we had been offered the company. I took immense pleasure in turning them down. This was going to be our business, mine and Kate's, nobody else's.

I wrote to Farmway thanking them for their offer, but announcing I had to decline it as I'd decided to purchase the business of Ray Green Animal Health. I knew they would be absolutely gutted because, as a bigger company, they took great pleasure in flexing their financial muscle. They had wanted me, and they had wanted Ray's business. They got neither – and from that moment on they tried every way they could to destroy my business.

I'd given notice to Jeff after seven years and began trading as Ray Green Animal Health at Easter on 13 April 2004. I worked on my own initially and Kate continued working for Jeff at Laycock's in Malton. We didn't exactly tell Jeff our plans. I'd given a month's notice and Jeff had put me on 'gardening leave' for that time. Kate stayed with Jeff for three months before joining me.

I had a shock that first day in Northallerton when I had to do a stocktake and realised that the figure we had put in to buy the business was just that – and now we needed to find £9,000 for the stock that was unsold in the shop. We were very naïve. It was the same kind of thing as buying the debt on the milk round, except we still had to sell this stock.

To get into perspective how far we have grown today I

have more than £9,000 worth of stock in my fridge behind the counter and at any given time our stock count will be approaching a quarter of a million pounds!

There was a really old Toyota Hiace van that came with the business, a quite low long thing. This bloody van was a nightmare. It would only just reach the top of Sutton Bank, one of North Yorkshire's steepest, windiest roads, with the radiator almost on the boil. Its back door wouldn't shut properly, so I had this bit of rope tied to the inside of the back seat to keep it shut.

I'd gone from my new Daihatsu Fourtrak and SEXY1 to this! But there's a lot you don't mind when it's your own business and you're building it up. We worked so hard and boy, did we take some business of Jeff. We knew so many people around the Malton and North York Moors, Wolds and Vale of Pickering area – and we also had Ray's existing customers in the Northallerton, Thirsk and Vale of York areas.

It was a big commute for Kate from Brompton by Sawdon near Scarborough to Northallerton – a round trip of 100 miles – and at this time it was a shorter one for me at Huby; but it was also brilliant because Kate could go back on an evening with supplies ready to deliver over there. We hung on to a lot of those customers.

We found a product to worm grouse, being manufactured by Peter Owen of Owen's Nutrition at Great Smeaton. It was a hit with gamekeepers and as we were buying it direct from a local source we did well from it. Peter also had this building and a forklift we rented as a warehouse, just a couple of miles from the shop, as we had quickly grown out of the bothy in the mart. Anywhere we could, we were buying in bulk to bring our cost per item down and the business was flying.

Peter sadly passed away but his son and daughter Andrew and Michelle still run the business and are a major supplier to us to this day.

Six months on from starting we rang up Judy, who had left Laycock's to have a baby, and asked whether she fancied a part-time job working two days a week in Malton. We knew what we were doing because she knew everybody. It wasn't so much even a bothy, more of a cupboard, but now we had two branches. I was at Northallerton 8 till 5, five days a week, with mart days on a Tuesday and Wednesday understandably being our most productive, and I delivered on a night.

For the first and only time in our business lives we were in the black. I couldn't believe it. We got rid of the old Toyota Hiace and I had a new Mercedes Sprinter. I remember writing the cheque out for it as we could afford it. We also changed the name, dropping Ray's name.

Unfortunately, he'd had a poor credit history and that had been a problem for us when getting new accounts with other businesses whose products we were hoping to sell.

After 12 months – in 2005, we became Green Farm Health.

Me and Dad
on the farm

Me and
Dad at
Scarborough

Me and
Grandad
Bob

Me and
Grandad
Bob with
Tommy

My first photo shoot!

At 7 years old with my first girlfriend Lesley in Benghazi

Mum, Dad holding my brother Andrew, me and Grandad Bob

In the Sahara Desert

Mum and Dad

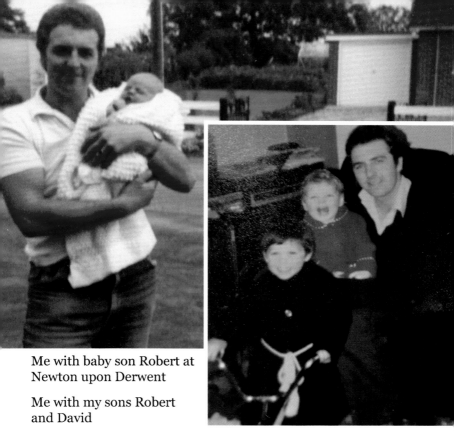

Me with baby son Robert at Newton upon Derwent

Me with my sons Robert and David

Robert, David, grandson William, me and Dad

Above: The Fab 4 :
across two pics. Top
– me, Stuart and Lyle
– Rob was taking pic.
Rob, me and Stuart –
Lyle was taking pic

On the Norfolk
Broads – a Fab
4 holiday to
remember!

On Komandoo, when I proposed to Kate

My Lady in Red on our wedding day!

Our First Kiss at
Aldwark Manor

On Barra, our
favourite island

Kate and me at work.
Do you need a Lazer
Tag?

With Richard Woolfe (*Celebs on the Farm* Executive Producer)

When Spring View Roxburgh sold for 2400 guineas at Carlisle in November 2017

On the farm with my beloved Whitebred Shorthorns

Me and Elsie the Oxford Sandy & Black pig famous for the AI episode on *The Yorkshire Vet* on Channel 5

Me and Julian (Norton) of *The Yorkshire Vet*
with Elsie's piglets

Filming *The Yorkshire Vet* at Spring View Farm

Celebs on the Farm – our farm sign. Here we go with Series 1!

Series 1 – The Celebs' first morning in the barn

Left: Me and Stephen – make your own caption!

Believe it or not, this cheeky shot was about shepherding sheep!

The day I sent
Megan home

Gleb &
Ashley at
the Pig Spa

Louis and Charlotte's last day

My first *Celebs on the Farm* Champion – Gleb Savchenko

CHAPTER 17

Meanwhile, Back in Huby

Time for a few bombshells. Time to cover off things at home that were taking place from 2002 onwards, including a pregnancy, a termination, an affair (not mine!), and a wife's sister (hmm). And once again, a huge debt and another terrible mess. These were the highlights, or lowlights, of what were to be my last four years with Diane as we, Kate and I shifted from being with Laycock's to starting Green's.

How Diane and I managed 10 years of marriage I just don't know. We simply carried on as though everything was okay, and it seemed alright at times, but it wasn't really.

The boys had left our home on Usher Lane in Haxby by November 2002 when Diane and I sold the house where I had lived for the past 13 years.

By now in 2002 they would be 23 and 22. Their uncle Robert, Donna's brother, had left them some money in his will. He'd always said that when he passed away everything he had would go to them. Robert's friend Jim also received a part of Robert's will, but Jim wrote that when he passed, whatever he has will also go to Robert and David. The initial monies they both received set them up nicely. They both now have their own homes and businesses.

I'd found Diane and I this detached 4-bedroomed house called Sunnyvale in Huby. It had a massive garden. Everything needed renovating – house and garden. It was very dilapidated. An old lady had lived there on her own.

It was a challenging project to bring it up to scratch, but I was up for it and so too was Diane.

Not long after we had moved in Diane dropped a bombshell. She was pregnant. I couldn't believe it. I really didn't want another child and certainly not with Diane. I was enraged, angry and unhappy. I don't know whether it was a mistake or whether Diane thought by getting pregnant our relationship would improve, but it knocked me for six.

I didn't know what to do. She knew I was totally against her having the baby and she decided to have a termination. I felt sick when she told me, but I knew it had been what I wanted and to me it was the right thing. Looking back, I feel terrible about this. I didn't ask Diane to have the termination, but she knew that I was so unhappy about the thought of being a parent again.

To be honest when I look back at my marriage to Diane I can't think of many happy, nice times. I'm sure there were lots of them, but it was almost like a non-event. We shouldn't have married. I never loved her – and maybe that showed more than ever over the pregnancy. That was probably the beginning of the end for us looking back.

We spent a lot of time and money on Sunnyvale, as we had on the house in Usher Lane, and with me also building the business at Laycock's all I really remember about the years around this time were simply eat, work, renovate, sleep, repeat.

We still got on alright and she did look after me and the home extremely well, but there was no real love, and now whatever passion there may have been wasn't there either. The pregnancy had put me off.

Somewhere between 2004, when Kate and I had bought Ray Green's business, and February 2006 my world took a few bizarre turns, one of which brought about the end of marriage number two.

Steven Osguthorpe and Sean Gell were friends and we often went out for a drink with them on a Friday night or met up and would go for a meal at The Blacksmith's Arms in Newton on Ouse. They were good blokes, mates. I'd known them for years and had originally met Steven when we were sheep dipping together. (Note to my good friend Stephen Bailey, I can see you smiling and raising your eyebrows. This is not a euphemism!). Diane had known Steven for years too.

Steven was a builder and joiner and Sean wasn't qualified but was also great at those kind of jobs. They were a good team and helped us with a lot of the work at Sunnyvale. Steven's brother Andy Osguthorpe was also a builder and we had an extension built with Diane and I doing a lot of the labouring work.

When we went out together we usually fell into a routine where Steven and I would talk together quite a bit; Diane would talk with Sean a lot.

Now before we get to where this eventually leads, because none of this is the bizarre bit just yet, but it's on its way, there was an incident.

Steven and Sean had built this wonderful big shed at the bottom of our massive garden. It really was pretty damned good, had a tiled roof and everything. It was better than a shed.

It was Diane's parents' golden wedding anniversary and we had all her family staying with us. It was party time and a lovely sunny autumn day. Diane's sister Helen had come up from London with her daughter Sabrina.

Helen was a physiotherapist, and when I found out, I somewhat suddenly developed symptoms of lower back pain! She had, very kindly and somewhat tenderly, been doing some exercises with me during the couple of days she was staying. You probably know where this is heading, but I didn't! Honestly!

Get this! We have all these people here, everyone's having tea and sandwiches in the middle of the afternoon, and I say, 'I'm just going to take some boxes down to the shed, get them out of the way,' and Helen said, 'I'll come and help.'

As we are wandering down to the end of the garden, she says, 'I've only got a little thong on under his dress you know, that's all.' I said, 'Really?' And I twanged it. Then I said, 'Look what you've done to me now.' Helen said, 'Oh yes.'

We opened the shed door. It has no windows. It might have been a great shed, but it still was a shed, thank God, no windows! Helen stood there and said, 'Don't you think I've a lovely body for a woman of my age?'

This is Diane's sister! It's her mother and father's golden wedding anniversary! And all Helen wanted was for me to shag her in the shed! I think we'll move on!

In early 2006 I discovered Diane was having an affair! Her mobile phone was on the kitchen table and had vibrated as I walked by. I'd never looked at it before, but I'd had my suspicions as she'd started going to work earlier than was really necessary. A message came up: 'Can't wait to see you tomorrow morning.' I read the other previous messages. I couldn't believe what I was reading. Meeting this guy in a hotel, graphic descriptions of what they'd been doing. I sent the message to my phone and put it down, thinking that's it. The marriage is over.

I knew we couldn't go on, and that night when she came home I told her we needed to talk. I said, 'You're having an affair.' I read the messages to her, after asking her to show me her phone. She said she'd been seeing him for three months. Was there any way we could work through this? I said no, absolutely no way. She packed all her things and moved out shortly afterwards. I was glad I'd discovered Di was having an affair because it got me out of a marriage I should never have been in.

This was now two wives who had had affairs. I remember thinking, 'How do I tell my sons?' I phoned them both and asked them to meet me in a local pub.

They were both so happy that this had happened! So far as they were concerned, they were going to get their dad back. What I hadn't realised was how much they disliked Diane.

Diane's affair didn't last, but then an even stranger happening took place months later. Steven (Osguthorpe) rang me in tears and asked to come and see me. Di had gone off with Sean! It's a crazy world! The boys had been together for 10 years!

But even that is not all. One thing I've never been brilliant with is the finances, particularly at home. I've always left the opening of letters, bills, invoices to each of my three wives, Donna, Diane and Kate – and when Di and I split I was about to find just how much debt I had!

Di had re-mortgaged the house. I'd had to sign it too, as we were both signatories, but look, I'm stupid I know, I'd just signed it blindly and we'd had this ridiculous mortgage going on at a ridiculous percentage with some dodgy company that I hadn't realised and credit cards that were totally maxed out. When Diane had left and I started opening the post, I soon became aware of the mess we had been in.

We were very lucky. We were able to sell Sunnyvale very quickly otherwise I would have been declared bankrupt and who knows what consequence that would have had for the business. I'm sure it would have finished me, but after everything had been paid off through the sale of the house, I came out with about £5,000. It could have been a lot worse.

And if that wasn't a crazy enough time, 2006 was about to get a whole lot crazier as I embarked on a few months of fun!

CHAPTER 18

Y Viva Espana

In April 2006 I moved to a one-bedroomed apartment above a former granary on a farm in Sheriff Hutton, appropriately called The Old Granary. The very nice couple who had a big house next door spent a lot of time away and wanted someone to be on the farm when they were away and clean up the meeting room below my apartment where church-type meetings were held. I could live there for free, in return for looking after the place. It was ideal.

I'm now 48, back single again, quite fit, healthy and still of course ravishingly good looking! The business was going really well. We were very busy, and I was happy that I was no longer with Diane. Life was good – and pretty soon it was to get very good, exciting and send me on another amazing adventure, meeting another beautiful woman. It's time for Senor Chris!

My boys, Robert and David, had planned a holiday to Magaluf in Mallorca with their mates in June, and they had asked me to go for a week. My brother Ian and his wife Anne came too, as did Andy Osguthorpe's son Luke and his girlfriend Laura. We took this lovely apartment where Robert, David and their mates had rented, which had a pool.

I'm abroad. I'm single. There's sun, sea, sand and, you know what normally comes next. Wait for it!

It was Father's Day while we were in Magaluf and that morning the boys told me they would have something sorted for me that night. Naïve or what! I just anticipated a few beers, nothing much more.

They took me to this place called Heaven – or to be more accurate, Heaven Lap Dancing Club! In we go, down these dark stairs. That bit looked a little seedy, but when we got downstairs it was quite nice with music playing, lights going, a lovely long glass bar – and this woman writhing around topless on this pole with nothing on but a tiny pair of knickers. Far from being full of old men, the place was full of younger people. I was probably the oldest person there. Hi-heeled women were walking around in skimpy tops. They all looked about 7ft tall.

David said, 'Dad, just choose one.' I asked him what he meant, and he elaborated, 'Choose one, go for a dance. It's your present.'

This gorgeous girl says, 'Hello darling, I am Camilla, from Russia. Would you like me to dance?' Camilla took me to a room. She sat on my lap, took her top off and gave me this 'dance' that lasted what seemed about 5 minutes. It was just amazing. I'd never experienced anything like it before. You have to put your hands under your bum. You're not allowed to touch, just for future reference if you're ever going to Magaluf!

As we were about to leave Camilla came over to me, gave me a peck on the cheek, held my hand and said, 'Thank you, darling,' as I'd bought her another drink after the 'dance'. In my hand she put a note saying, 'Camilla, call me,' with her mobile number.

Of course, I called her! The next day. We met for lunch and a glass of wine in a restaurant in Palma Nova. She looked gorgeous in the daytime, very tall and willowy with long auburn hair. She was 28 and from Ukraine.

When I told the others – Ian and Anne and Luke and Laura – that I was going to ask Camilla to come to the apartment, as I had my own room, they went mad. They were hiding their passports in the fridge, hiding their money and when I asked what they were doing it for, they said she was clearly coming to nick things. She never did come to the apartment, but I did keep seeing her and we had a fantastic time. Sunbeds in the middle of the night can be useful things you know!

I packed a lot into that week and had such a wonderful time with Robert and David, their mates, Ian and my crowd, and Camilla. And we had another 'incident' too, this time nothing to do with me but a proper bust up when Steven and Sean arrived later. This was before Di and Sean had shacked up and involved a bit of a fracas that saw off a bed, balcony railings and a door, that led to Luke and I going in to Palma Nova to buy screws, wood and paint to mend what had been trashed by certain individuals.

Now you might think this thing with Camilla wouldn't last. Wrong. I spent much of the rest of the year flying back to Mallorca with everybody telling me I was losing it, or words to that effect. Okay, they said, 'You're f***ing crackers.' But I didn't give a f***. I was enjoying this. I had some money. I had no mortgage to pay. The business was doing well and I was on my own. So far as I was concerned, I felt like James Bond and she was my Russian Bond girl.

I know how crazy all of this sounds, but I was in this bubble, having a wonderful time. I'd come out of a bad marriage. I was living on my own in this apartment and I'd found this girl who for whatever reason, and I wasn't really bothered what the reason was, liked me. We had a great time together, both sexually and romantically. And she was good fun.

By now I knew Camilla's real name – Oksana – and she knew this restaurant in Puerto Portals, home of the most glamorous marina on the island and a very plush resort. Joan Collins was staying in Puerto Portals at the time. The restaurant was beautiful, magical with spurts of water blowing up and a fan that blew mist over to keep you cool. This was also the only time I have ever eaten sushi.

It was bloody outrageous too! This was and still remains the most expensive lunch I have ever bought! She chose the finest wine and a fish dish for two, followed by a delicious ice cream dessert. The bill – a mere 150 Euros! OMG! But I didn't care. There I was lunching in a fabulous restaurant with this gorgeous willowy young Russian girl. Amazing.

How mad was this, to a normal person at any rate. I once flew out to be with Oksana for the night and flew back the next morning.

The killer came when she rang one day asking for money. This was what my friends had thought all along, that there would come a time. Oksana said, 'Darling, my mother needs 2000 Euros, can you help me?' I was tempted to let her have it, as I knew that would guarantee another wonderful time together, but I decided that was enough. And Oksana fell out with me.

We kept in touch for a short while, but I'd felt our time had been coming to its natural end anyway. I'd had a wonderful time with this wonderful young lady, but that was it.

The following year I was back over in Magaluf with friends and asked after her, through a few of her friends I'd got to know during our time together. She'd gone to live in Paris – with her daughter! OMG!

Oksana had had a baby! I never saw her again. Looking back maybe that's what she'd wanted the money for and maybe wanted to move to England, but I thought to myself I'd had my time. You're 48 Chris, she's 28. It's over.

But even that wasn't enough for me! Oh no! I am fairly ashamed to say that I have also slept with a prostitute, but again, it really wasn't my fault! It was on one of my jaunts to Magaluf in or around 2006. I think I'd gone on a long stag weekend with my brother Ian, my two lads and quite a few others, and of course we were lads being lads.

We were in one of our favourite bars, 'Crusoe's', right on the front and being quite boisterous. It was mid-afternoon and very hot. This amazingly stunning blonde joined us. She had just arrived from Ibiza and announced she was 'partying around the Balearics'. She had the most incredible breasts and was wearing skimpy shorts and a bikini top. We had a good laugh with her. That was it really. Until a knock on my door about 8pm as I was getting ready to go out with everyone for the night.

OMG it was her. Some twat in our group had discovered what she did for a living and had given her my hotel details. Well, I tried to get out of this but look, I had just got out of the shower, she was incredibly sexy, and she started to well, you know ... and then said it would be 200 Euros! Wow! No way!

I said, 'I'm sorry love, I don't pay for this.' We settled on 50 Euros and off she went into the night. It was all over so quickly. I felt really upset I had paid for sex! Anyway, I soon got over it and got a fair bit of ribbing later that night from the bastards who were supposedly my mates!

And then this other woman came into my life, briefly, the same year. She was one of our suppliers. We would talk on the phone, a bit flirty and she said she would love to meet me. We met on a couple of occasions! Clearly 2006 must have been my gap year, sowing wild oats, enjoying my freedom!

By December 2006 the nice couple who were letting me stay rent free must have realised I was probably spending as much time away from the farm, and meeting room, as they were, and they very pleasantly ended our agreement. I'd not been very comfortable there, nothing to do with the apartment. It just wasn't me, and I wasn't really cut out to be a caretaker.

Where next? Time for Dog-loving Chris!

CHAPTER 19

Pip

Magaluf wasn't the only place I was spending a lot of time in 2006. The all-new Thirsk Farmers Auction Market was to open in September.

Now you might think, from the last chapter, that this year was all about me just having a wild time but there was still my sensible, business head and I knew a move to this fantastic new rural centre could be the making of us.

When we first went to see the unit, it was just a breezeblock shell with a concrete floor. It was the biggest unit they had, and Kate said we couldn't afford it. I said we couldn't not afford to have it. If we were going to take our business to the next stage we had to go there. The only other option was to stay where we were in the bothy, but where was that going?

We negotiated really hard, ensuring there was a clause in the deal that meant we were the sole providers of all animal health products on the site, received three months' free rent and went from a tiny bothy of 8ft x 4ft to 3000sq ft of new premises that needed offices, shelving, painting and a huge amount of stock. It was a massive undertaking! There's no wonder I looked forward to my little jaunts over to Magaluf to see Oksana.

We'd worked with HSBC since we had started two years previously and they supported us wonderfully as they have all along. They organised a business loan to kit the place out as we ploughed our profits back in.

Shortly after we moved in, I drove to work one day, rolled up into the car park, and saw this huge sign at the front saying FARMWAY!

I saw red! I was livid! Even though we had negotiated with our new landlords they had let a small unit at the front of the premises to Farmway, my arch rivals ever since turning them down and acquiring Ray's business. Farmway had spent all weekend filling their place up with animal health products. I met with the mart directors and they told me Farmway weren't stocking animal health products. I showed them they were.

By that time I had found out what Farmway had done. These were all dummy packs. They had somehow been able to take advantage of what was written in the contract and were not actually stocking physical product on the site, but customers could go in to their unit, order and they would send the customer half a mile away to pick up his or her order. I told the mart directors that defeated the whole object of why we had moved there.

If I'd been livid when I'd first seen that Farmway had been allowed to take a unit, after we had been so specific, it was nothing compared to the day I went absolutely berserk!

We had planned an open day shortly after we had moved in, so that we could own the event, we were using the rest of the market premises including the main entrance hall and the mart café was open. We even had a band on. We'd arranged it on a non-market day, so that we could do this. We'd sent out hundreds of invitations. It was our event.

Farmway only opened on a market day and you can guess the rest. They opened their doors on our open day! I was ballistic with rage! How dare they!

In fairness to the mart directors they saw exactly what Farmway were doing and this act really sorted everything out for us. They told Farmway to leave and our bitter rivals received their notice. It worked out well for us in the end, but it also showed me the extent people and rival businesses would go to.

Ian Woodhead, who is chairman of the mart, Harry his father and Alan Armstrong, all mart directors, were very much behind us and we have a great relationship still today. We have continued to grow, taking more space and we kept on the bothy at Northallerton too. With Judy at Malton and taking on Mike Foster and Anna Simpson, as she was called then, for Thirsk, and sending who we could to man the bothy at Northallerton, we had a great team.

We gradually took on more staff and the decision to move into Thirsk Mart was vindicated. If we hadn't taken it on, we probably wouldn't have been in business today – and we wouldn't have bought a farm, I wouldn't have appeared on *The Yorkshire Vet* and I wouldn't have become Farmer Chris on *Celebs on the Farm*. Funny old world!

Our stock being carried was now suddenly around £100,000 in value. We were in a position of overtrading which is very dangerous. It happens when you expand too quickly without having the financial resources to support it. It's all about working capital and cash flow. Sales were going up and up, but because of the retail business we run customers have credit accounts and that means you're giving free credit, yet you're having to pay suppliers before you get paid for what you have sold.

Sales are great, but cash is king and without the right kind of cash flow you are screwed. We didn't get into trouble, but with sales going up every month and still as a relatively new business, we didn't keep our eye on the profit margin as much as we should.

Credit control and profit margin are hugely important and so we matched our push for greater sales with harder credit control and putting our prices up where we could. Kate and I have always handled credit control and we are pretty tight.

It was a very hard and tough time for Kate and I business wise, but as much as I was having my crazy year, so too was Kate. Not the same as mine, although she was also coming out of a marriage.

Kate left her husband in the summer of 2006 and moved into a rented cottage in the lovely little North York Moors village of Gillamoor. I was stunned! I'd had no idea this was going to happen. They had been married for 25 years.

She was like a new woman! I think her marriage with David had been most unhappy and the new lease of life the business had given her had inspired her to leave him and start a new life.

Our relationship had always been good. She's a real country girl, loves riding and hunting and one of her passions was showing sheep at agricultural shows, especially the Great Yorkshire, and as I was to discover later, this was also a good excuse to get away with friends and party.

Kate and I had always worked closely together right from when I first started at Laycock's. We'd flirted. She kind of knew everything that was going on in my life, well maybe not everything. I'm sure I didn't tell her I was popping over to Magaluf every time I actually did so that year, but we were two people who had worked together initially and then had gone into business together, so we automatically had a responsibility to each other if something was going wrong in our personal lives and we could help.

I'd like to think I've helped Kate as much as she has helped me, but I know it has probably been a bit the other way around at times – and it certainly was in early December 2006 when Kate found me this place in the square in the centre of Easingwold, a lovely old market town between York and Thirsk. By then my Magaluf-hopping and the times with Oksana were over, we'd been concentrating on the business and we were doing great. Sales were good and increasing all the time. I'd come down to earth a little bit, or as far as my natural personality allows.

I moved into Driffield House in Easingwold on December 6, 2006. I was renting. It was an end cottage, two-bedroomed with a little garden. Kate helped me. We moved everything I owned, which comprised two van loads of belongings and Kate said, 'I'm going to buy you a dog.' She got me Pip, a little Jack Russell terrier not even a year old, from one of her friends. Kate said, 'She'll be really good for you, someone to be there for when you're home.' And Kate was right.

I loved this little dog. Pip and I became inseparable.

CHAPTER 20

Kate – The Start

Kate and I were both now separated from our marital partners and our business was going well. We were working closely together and my new place in Easingwold was less than 10 miles from where we had our business in Thirsk livestock market. It made sense for Kate to stay over after we'd had a meal in a local pub or restaurant, and that's when we first slept together.

After a few months we just thought this is silly, why are we renting separate places? Why not pool our resources and rent just one? We found a lovely cottage in the village of Crayke, just a couple of miles from Easingwold, with a big garden for Pip and Kate's dog Tillie and moved in May 2007. We rented The Old Cottage in Main Street, went to the very famous pub in the village The Durham Ox, walked the dogs together and enjoyed meals out at 'The Ox'.

Mike and Sasha Ibbotson own the Durham Ox and are really rather good at what they do! They've won loads of awards. This became our local haunt and we met many friends there including 'Stan' Featherstone, Andrew Warriner and Rob Dawson who are still customers now, a lovely couple called Neil and Bev, Mick and Carol Powton and many others. It is still a favourite venue and we always return for our wedding anniversary meals on our 'special table'.

One other nice thing about the Durham Ox is its beautiful private dining room with adjoining lounge. We have a 'gang' who meet here every January. It all started at my 50th birthday event. Kate and I, Robert and Sally Dent, brother Ian and wife Ann, Stuart and Barbara Smallwood, Dave and Barbara Medd, Andy and Christine Osguthorpe, Lyle and Christine, Richard and Fran Newby, and of course Richard and Janet Taylor. We have such a lovely, convivial evening which usually results in several sore heads the next day! Long may it continue.

Back to where we had got to. Moving in to Crayke.

Kate and I were really happy. I was particularly happy too, because as we were renting, I didn't have to do anything to the property.

We were on the up at Green's. As we had more storage space it gave us a lot more scope. I was on the lookout for new business all the time. We were stocking more animal feed and bulkier items. We'd branched out into field gates, livestock handling equipment and we had bought another vehicle, employing a driver for deliveries.

Kate's divorce settlement eventually came through. It had been a little protracted because of the property she and David had lived in and proved a bit complicated, but she ended up with a little bit of money from it and she wanted to buy a house.

Remember I've nothing, apart from what is in the business and we're using that to expand. Farmers are prone to paying very slowly, so you're always making a profit on paper, as we have done every year, but you're also always in the red, not the black. Any money I've had, I've blown on lap dancing and extra curricula activities in my 'gap year'.

Consequently, I'm not as up for purchasing a house because (a) I'm not contributing to it as I have no money of my own; and (b) I was worried about property prices at the time and thought they would come down. I'd already been the victim of negative equity years before and I didn't want that again.

But Kate was adamant. She hated paying rent and

wanted to put money into property. We were coming back from a Sunday morning walk when she got quite emotional, there were tears, and she said she really wanted to buy this house we'd seen in Husthwaite, another pretty village close by.

I didn't want to buy it, but I thought who am I to say no? I said, 'You've the money, Kate, I haven't. If you want me to come with you, let's do it.'

In October 2008 we moved into Wortley Cottage in The Nookin in Husthwaite, using Kate's settlement as a deposit and taking on a mortgage together, but even though I'd said let's do it, I still felt under duress. I didn't like it.

The cottage was old, dark and damp. It's not where I wanted to live, but it was Kate's money that had enabled us to move and I felt like I was part of the package and that I needed to be supportive. We had become a couple in life, as well as in business.

If I'd thought Sunnyvale had been a project, this beat it hands down. It needed so much work. The garden was a forest, the heating didn't work properly, a new boiler was needed, the bathroom needed replacing and the damp proof needed doing.

And then there was Sally!

I was back in this weird place, a really bad place in my head. Maybe it was about not having my own money to put into a house, maybe it was because I felt I hadn't been able to put in my share, I definitely hadn't wanted to buy the house. I think maybe I had felt trapped by it all, that I hadn't had a choice and I'd had to move here because of us being in business together.

Whatever it was, I could have left Kate to the house and I could have left the business behind just at that moment.

I used to spend time at our local village pub in Husthwaite, because I was a bit fed up. This girl was working there. She was very fanciable and it all started with a kiss in the car park. It didn't go on very long. We had a night in Leeds. I'd told Kate I was going on a stag weekend. We had a few good times.

Hands up, I enjoyed it while it lasted and I know it was probably make or break for Kate and I, but at the time I still had this ridiculous silly bubble that said fuck the house, fuck work, I've a nice car – I'd just got a new Land Rover Discovery – and I'm having a good time. It's bad, but that's how I felt.

The moment of truth for me didn't come from Kate, who is not daft by any means and probably knew exactly what was going on – remember she had known me for years, but from a couple of old pals. One of them said about Sally, to me, 'Can you not see that word TROUBLE tattooed on her forehead?' Apparently, she was having an affair with a married man. And then another person, a farmer said, 'Hey Sid (using my name from all those years ago, like I said it has stuck) I've a right tart, she's a right one.' It was Sally.

That was when I came to my senses. I ended it, dropped her, and that is when Kate and I began seriously becoming the couple we have been ever since, the couple we are today – married, farming together, in business together and a great partnership in every way. Kate is my rock.

CHAPTER 21

The Worst Year of My Life

Our business is very busy approaching Christmas and we sell around 500 Christmas trees, as well as all the other items involved with a busy Country Store. December is a long hard month and by the end of it we are both ready for a break as we work every day and try and give our team as much time off as possible.

We used to treat ourselves to a 10-night holiday in the Caribbean in January, this was before we bought Spring View Farm, and in 2008 we flew out to Barbados.

It was a lovely holiday and when we returned home we were ready to get stuck into work again with lots of new ideas and plans. Little did we know this was going to be the worst 12 months of our lives.

Wednesday, late afternoon, about 4 pm just after we had returned from Barbados, I was about to take our two dogs for a walk before we left the store at 5pm. A police officer came into the store. He told me a complaint had been made and he needed to talk to me in private. I put the dogs into the pickup and met him in our office.

When we had both sat down he said that the complaint had been made against me. I asked what complaint in particular, thinking had we done something to upset a competitor business.

He said the complaint was from a woman who claimed I had touched her in this very office. I immediately asked Kate to join us. I asked him to repeat what he had said. I was bewildered, shocked, upset and felt sick. He informed me that I was not being arrested but I had to go to the police station on the following Friday afternoon to be interviewed. If I didn't, he would arrest me and take me.

Kate went white and asked who it was that had made the complaint. He wouldn't say. He left us with a strict instruction that I had to be at the police station at 3pm on Friday. This was so shocking to us both. Neither of us has ever had anything to do with a police investigation and certainly not one involving this type of thing. We went home terrified, couldn't eat or sleep, and spent most of the night wondering who it was.

We both found it difficult to work or concentrate on anything. I was told to get a solicitor to attend with me on Friday, if not there would be a duty solicitor there. I contacted our solicitor and he said he was sorry, but he didn't do criminal cases, 'You will have to find someone else.'

Criminal? I couldn't believe what he said. I'm not a criminal! He gave me the number of someone he knew, and I arranged to meet them at the police station.

I had never been in a police station before. There was someone behind a counter and I explained I was there to be interviewed. Eventually my solicitor turned up and we were shown through to the interview area. I had to stand in front of the duty sergeant, have my photo taken and fingerprints. I signed several forms. This was truly awful. Then we were shown into a room adjacent to the duty sergeant which had clear glass partitions so he could see what we were doing but not hear. Then I was told about disclosure. This is when the prosecutor gives the defendant the information they have about the alleged offence. The police officer brought in his file, gave it to my solicitor and left us.

The complaint was from a female who had visited my business in early December and had given a written statement saying that I had touched her bottom, over her trousers, in the office at my business.

We had to read through the whole statement and prepare my response for a recorded interview. I had no idea where to start. I remembered this person being in the office, but not a lot about the conversation we had. I simply couldn't believe what I was looking at on the statement. They were all lies!

We then had to go into a soundproofed room with the police officer. He spoke very firmly and told us he was starting the interview and there were 3 CD's in the recording machine to record every word that was said. I mean I was terrified now! This is something you see on the telly. Not me. Surely not me?

The interview went on for around 15 minutes. There wasn't really much I could do but deny everything. I didn't even know what the alleged offence was or who had made it until I got there that Friday.

The police officer said he would be in touch if he needed further information and I returned home shell-shocked. I was so worried I couldn't sleep. The offence I had allegedly committed was 'sexual touching' and of course this was very serious.

Negative, horrible things have a habit of getting out and I knew people were talking about me. This was most distressing for Kate and I. We didn't sleep properly, eat or enjoy anything. Every waking moment this was in our heads. What was going to happen?

My solicitor wasn't helping. I wanted to know more but I couldn't get hold of him when I needed to.

My good friend Jonathan 'Jonners' Reay, who I'd confided in, told me he knew of a very good solicitor who specialised in cases like this and he put me in touch with him. Thank goodness he did as he was excellent. A huge thank you to 'Jonners', you are a real friend.

I then had a call from the police officer to return for a

further interview. The same procedure as last time, only this time it was to answer claims from another woman that I had touched her too!

Again, this was the most awful experience and I couldn't wait to get home. I just wanted to run away, this was so awful. I felt sick all day and night. Kate felt the same.

Driving to work on a morning with the radio on and a favourite piece of music might come on, but I would turn it off because I felt I just couldn't smile or enjoy any pleasures while this investigation was going on.

The police officer had interviewed two male members of staff who were at work that day of the alleged offence, but crucially not the female member who was actually working there that day also.

We heard nothing for months and were beginning to think that perhaps things weren't going any further. People we spoke to were reassuring at the time, telling us not to worry because if anything was going to happen we would have heard by now.

In mid-summer I got a call from one of the male members of staff who had been interviewed. He told me the investigating police officer had phoned him, left a message on his voice mail to say the case had been dropped and he wouldn't be needed anymore. Hallelujah!

This was the best news I could wish for and at last I had a smile on my face! I told Kate and we were so relieved.

As the day went on, I wondered why the police officer hadn't called me himself? I called and asked why he had called my witness but not me? His reply made me fall to the floor in disbelief.

He told me he had a lot of cases on at the time and he must have left the wrong person the message. My case was ongoing. We were back to feeling sick and distressed once more.

Late summer the police officer phoned to say the CPS were going to charge me for the offence raised by the first complainant, but that the second one had been dropped. I would hear from their prosecution team in due course.

We had just returned back to Worley Cottage after a day at the annual sheep sale at Wombleton in October when a big brown envelope with CPS stamped on it had arrived. Trembling, I opened it and it stated the charges. I had to appear at magistrates' court to answer them.

I now knew I was going to court. I went into deep anxiety and feelings of depression. It really was the most awful time for both of us. Imagine what a field day the press would have? And what about our business? But most important of all – I hadn't done anything!

I met with my new solicitor to prepare my defence and told him everything that had happened. He was a most experienced solicitor who specialised in this sort of thing. The case was due to be heard at the end of the month, but he told me he couldn't be there as he was on holiday!

He would send a barrister he knew. The day arrived and my old mate Stuart said he would take me and stay with me. He knew I was terrified. My barrister arrived. She and I went into a room to discuss what was going to happen.

My solicitor had advised me to go into the Magistrates Court, plead 'not guilty' and ask for it to be referred to Crown Court. There was an option to plead guilty here and now and get away with a fine and a warning.

There was never a chance I was going to plead guilty to something I hadn't done! My solicitor told me he felt the Crown Court would offer a better chance of me being proved not guilty.

We went in. There were three magistrates sat up high and me below. There were many other people in there too but I'm not sure what for. In front of me to my left was the prosecutor. She had a laptop in front of her. My barrister stood in front of me to my right. My name was read out. I was asked to confirm it and also my address. Then the prosecutor started to explain my alleged offence.

I was asked how I pleaded. 'Not Guilty,' I replied very firmly. The three pushed back on their chairs, going into some kind of huddle, whispering to each other. The head magistrate then announced that my case would now be referred to Crown Court next April. That was it. Less than 5 minutes.

I thanked the barrister and Stuart took me home. I now had 6 months of hell before appearing at Crown Court. Or so I thought.

A week later I received a letter from the CPS telling me I had to appear at Teesside Crown Court for a pre-trial hearing the following week!

My solicitor arranged for a barrister to come from Leeds. I didn't even want Kate to know about this. I hadn't told Mum and Dad, who were elderly and would be so worried. I did tell Kate of course, but I insisted she wasn't to come. I didn't want to put her through that experience.

My case was due at 10am but I was there at 9am. I was truly terrified. There really were some dreadful looking people here, waiting to go into court and most of them were laughing, joking and treating it like any other day!

This was the worst day of my life!

My solicitor arrived, took me into a meeting room and my barrister was there too, a lady barrister and she explained what would happen. An usher came for me and took me to the doors to the court. My solicitor and barrister followed. The wooden double doors opened, and we stood there looking in as the previous case, using a video link, was finishing.

The usher led us in. I had to go to the dock on the left where a security guard met me. My solicitor and barrister took their seats. I climbed several steps to the dock and the guard showed me through a door and closed it. He told me he was meant to strip search me, but because I was only there to enter a plea he wouldn't, and just ran a hand-held device over me to check for weapons. He then showed me out and I stood in the dock.

I looked up to the judge who was reading. To my left were 12 empty chairs with a bench in front of them. The jury area. There were many others in the court, all were either busy writing or reading something.

One of them stood up and asked my name and address. The judge then said, 'You are here to answer the charge of sexual assault on a female. How do you plead?'

Sexual ASSAULT? How had this gone from 'sexual touching' to assault? Not that I was guilty of either! I wanted to say something but thought better of it. 'Not guilty,' I replied. He then announced the date for my trial which was to be April 15, 2009. That was it. Another 5 minutes! But 5 minutes of pure hell for me. At least I was able to go home, but when was all this madness going to end?

My solicitor wasn't at all happy with the way this was going. He certainly didn't want me to face trial, although in his opinion I stood a far better chance with a jury than with magistrates, because in his opinion the magistrates would probably have gone against me.

We sat down the next week and went through everything. I asked him why the female member of staff hadn't been interviewed by the police, as she was a key witness.

The CCTV was of no use as the alleged offence took place in early December 2007 and wasn't reported till the end of January 2008, which meant our files were wiped. They only last a few weeks.

My solicitor spoke with the CPS and explained we

had a key witness we would bring to trial whom the police had not interviewed. The following week we received communication from them to ask my solicitor to accompany the female witness to the local police station to be interviewed by the CPS.

This finally took place and she was able to give them new information which absolutely clarified my version of events and made it impossible for the alleged offence to have taken place at the time and place the complainant had stated.

Christmas came and went. We heard nothing. I had decided we needed to go away and had booked for Kate and I to go on a break to the Dominican Republic in mid-January. We had just returned to work around January 3 and my solicitor phoned.

'Chris, I have just heard from the CPS. They are dropping the case as they know they have insufficient evidence to secure a conviction.'

I asked him to explain what this meant. He said that it meant it was all over. He had an email from the prosecutor stating this, and I would be receiving a letter that week explaining the case was dropped. I was so relieved I cried.

Talk about a millstone around your neck that has been removed! I wanted to cry again, I was so happy, but part of me now was also so angry.

Kate and I had endured 12 months of living hell, not knowing from one week to the next if I was going to be locked up for something I did not do and living in total fear of phone calls, letters and rumours.

Now it was over, but not because I had been proved not guilty, oh no, but because they had insufficient evidence. This still makes me angry to this day.

There was to be another twist. Just after my solicitor phoned with the news, Kate's friend Fiona rang: 'Chris you need to come to Scarborough Hospital. Kate has fallen off her horse and is injured.' I mean you couldn't make this up, could you? Kate had hurt her back and the paramedics were putting her on a stretcher with a neck brace. She needed an X-ray as they were worried about her spine.

I told Fiona my news and asked her to tell Kate the case had been dropped. I hoped it may help. I set off in the car towards Scarborough, got as far as Kirkbymoorside when Fiona rang again saying Kate was on her way back to her house.

Thank God she was OK – a bit different to what happened to her a few years later! Bloody horses, I thought. Kate was very sore and bruised but had no long-term injury.

We were both elated this awful business was at last over. The next week we received the official letter from the CPS stating the reasons the case was now dropped. I wanted them to go and arrest the people that made these false allegations, but of course that wasn't going to happen.

We enjoyed our holiday, but there was no celebration. This was the most dreadful experience of my life and it was going to take a lot more than a holiday to get over it.

CHAPTER 22

The Maldives

In January 2010 Kate and I had our first wonderful holiday in the Maldives but it didn't exactly start out the way I had planned.

I'd been to the travel agents and said I'd like to go to the Maldives, but I didn't want to go to a quiet island. What is wrong with me! The Maldives is mostly about romance, tranquillity, not loud and brash, but I didn't know that at the time, and because I'd asked for the kind of place that was not quiet, we got somewhere that felt like we were back in fucking Blackpool!

We had booked 10 nights in Kuredu. We'd flown from Manchester to Male international airport. That in itself was incredible. We then took a seaplane to Kuredu. Woah! Again fantastic. An amazing experience. We landed, as you do, in the sea and got off on to the jetty. But that's where I thought no, no, no, what have we come to? Kids running about all over the place, ice cream sellers, this wasn't what I'd had in mind at all. We hadn't been there an hour when I said to Kate, 'We shan't be coming back here.' There were massive discos going on. When I said I'd wanted something lively I hadn't meant this.

We went to the welcome meeting the next day. We never go to one of those. Well, I say we went to it. We were an hour late. The Maldives is five hours in front of the UK when you're on Male, but what you don't realise, or we didn't, is that Kuredu was another hour in front, so we missed the meeting!

But we did manage to speak to the rep. And good news

was about to come our way! The rep told us Kuredu was over-booked, with more people due in. Who does that kind of thing? There was a sister island called Komandoo, would we be interested in moving there?

I wasn't about to trade what we had for potentially something even worse, so I asked her to give us half an hour. I rang Mike at work and asked him to google Komandoo and let us know what he thought.

We had touched Gold! Mike rang back and said, 'Go! It's 5-star and it's amazing. Only 60 bungalows on the island that is just 500 metres long by 50 metres wide.' He said, 'Ask them for a water bungalow.'

Half an hour by boat and we were there. Paradise. Absolutely unbelievable. The most amazing place. Lovely restaurant in the middle of this miniscule island, palm trees, sunset bar on the beach. We taught ourselves to snorkel, swam with turtles, the most incredible relaxing holiday. Heaven on earth.

CHAPTER 23

Something Very Sad That Turned into Something Very Happy

Pip was the little daughter I'd never had. I adored this little dog. Kate had been so right about what Pip would do for me – and as she was such a lovely dog, we decided to have her mated.

Kate and I were continually building our business, opening new outlets; and we'd transformed Wortley Cottage. This was the place I didn't like initially, but it was actually a beautiful old cottage and with the work we had done renovating it we really did turn it into a lovely home. The glass roof we had put in over the patio made it a stunning place to sit on an evening with a bit of music going. It was sheltered and south-west facing which really caught the afternoon and early evening sun. Pip would always be with us.

Walking Pip had always been one of my favourite pastimes and when she was getting close to having her puppies I would take her into work with me. This particular day I had taken her for a walk at lunchtime. She bent to have a wee, or at least that's what I'd thought. I then realised, oh my God, you're not, you're having a puppy!

What do I do now? Kate wasn't there, she'd gone out delivering. I rang her and said she'd better get herself back as Pip was having her puppies – and so was I!

Kate got back just in time and Pip had four. We got her home and she and we had a lovely time with them. She reared them well and we sold them to good people.

All was good.

Not long after the pups had gone Pip wasn't very well and I was really worried. She was losing weight, she wasn't drinking, we couldn't get her to eat and she was lethargic. We took her to Howells, the vets in Easingwold, and they did some blood tests. Her condition was Haemolytic Anaemia. It is brought about when the immune system attacks the red blood cells. There is no cure.

My mum had just lost her brother in Hull and I was taking her over to deal with some affairs, but my mind was really with Pip who was at Howells. I was dreading the news.

On the way I received a call from the vets saying that I needed to make a decision about Pip. I knew what they meant. It was heartbreaking. Mum was understandably upset about what she was having to do, and so was I over the decision I knew had to be made. And really there was no decision. It just had to be done.

I had sunglasses on that day and driving back I had tears streaming down my face coming out of Hull on the way back home. Mum was talking away, but it was like when you see one of those TV scenes where you see people talking but can't hear them. I'd worn the shades so Mum couldn't see my eyes. I got Mum home, then went to see Kate. We had Pip put to sleep.

It was awful. She was just five years old, my baby and I loved her to bits. That day was so emotional. Pip had always gone in the back of my Land Rover Discovery. I carried her out of the vets in a blanket. Kate and I drove home. I dug a hole in the garden and buried her, crying my eyes out, as I am again writing this. That was Pip's last journey. I buried her with her little jumper.

I used to go to Pip's grave and I would put a blanket over it to keep her warm. I grieved for her that much. Kate and I had had a painting commissioned of Pip and every night I'd take the painting and just kiss her. I know it sounds silly. That's just how much I missed her.

There was one thing that came out of this that turned into something so strong. Kate and I were together in our grief.

This made me realise something so powerful – that I truly loved Kate. She'd put up with me, she'd put up with my meanderings, she cared for me. I realised at this time just how much I loved her.

CHAPTER 24

Mrs Jeffery the Third

I'd bought Kate jewellery for birthdays and at Christmas in the past, but after Pip had gone and with my feelings now so strong for her, I wanted to do something really special. My first thought was to buy something to thank her for all the support she had given me over Pip, but it was more than that, I wanted to show not just my thanks but how I felt about her, how she had become a part of me.

Kate chose a lovely ring, called a friendship ring, and wore it on her third finger of her right hand.

After having such a lovely time on Komandoo the previous January we booked again for 2011. This time we couldn't fly to Male airport as the direct flight to the Maldives we'd used in 2010 had stopped, so we flew instead to Doha in Qatar and then to Male where we took the seaplane, this time direct to Komandoo. This was another amazing experience as the island is so small it has a floating platform a couple of hundred metres long off the island and a tiny little boat comes out to pick up the visitors.

Kate and I were the only ones getting off the seaplane and when you reach the jetty you are greeted with the islanders walking down the jetty in front of you with flower petals. You enter a straw-roofed reception area with guitars being played by Maldives musicians, you're given fresh cool towels for your head and a gorgeous cocktail to take to your bungalow. It truly is an incredible feeling.

We had booked a beach bungalow this time, Turtle No 6, where you could walk into the lagoon, there was a huge bed in the room and everywhere smelt absolutely gorgeous, as though you were in a 24-hour spa. It was just as stunning, if not more so, than our first time, only this time I had a plan. I wanted to do something on this holiday. We'd been there nine out of the 10 nights before I plucked up the courage.

It was about 4 o'clock in the afternoon, the sun was getting lower in the sky and it is dusk by around 6 o'clock. We were all on our own on this little part of this beautiful little island. This paradise island. It was an idyllic evening by the gentle, warm shores of the Indian Ocean, the sea lapping out our feet with the breeze softly blowing.

I took one of the beach chairs we would sit in by the bungalow and put it on the edge of the ocean and asked Kate to come and sit on my knee. We were coming to the end of another wonderful, relaxing holiday. I put my arms around her. We looked out to the sea. It was one of those moments you could just cry, thinking about having to leave this wonderful place, so lovely, so calm and serene.

My moment had come.

I took hold of the friendship ring she'd chosen just a few months previously and it just slipped off. I said, 'Crikey, that's loose,' and Kate said, 'Yes, I must have lost a bit of weight. I must get it seen to when we get back.' I said, 'You must, I was just twiddling it and it came off.'

The next part of my plan.

To put it back on I took hold of Kate's left hand. I put it on the third finger of her left hand. Kate said, 'You've put it on the wrong finger,' and I said, 'No I haven't.' I stood up from the chair, went down on one knee in the Indian Ocean, looked at her and said, 'Kate, will you marry me?' It was the most romantic thing I've ever done.

And Kate said, 'You daft bugger, what are you saying?' I said it again as she was stunned and really had not expected this. When she said, 'Of course I will,' as she put her arms around me it was the most magical, lovely moment in the most magical, wonderful place in the world.

24 September 2011 was our wedding date and after looking around various venues we settled on Aldwark Manor not far from Easingwold. It suited exactly the kind of countryside environment where we both wanted to be married. When we had been researching where to go our good friends Dave and Barbara Medd came with us – Dave had trained me as a milkman for Northern Dairies – and we tried the hotel's wedding taster menu. We had braised blade of beef and Dave said he'd never ever tasted beef as good as that. My dad loved beef, so we ordered that as our main course for the wedding.

Kate loved organising the wedding and was determined to get married as the lady in red. She had this beautiful red dress that I of course wasn't allowed to see until the day itself, and it was stunning. She looked lovely. All of our close friends, family and work colleagues, who are all close friends too, were all with us on the day. We invited around 60 altogether. My gang were all there. The Fab 4. Stuart (Smallwood) with his wife Barbara; Rob (Dent) and Sally his wife; and Lyle with his partner Christine.

The night before the wedding we had a family meal at Aldwark Manor, where nearly everyone stayed except Kate, Fiona and her daughter, Mary, who was Kate's maid of honour. They went back to Wortley Cottage in Husthwaite. All my family and Kate's were at the meal including my boys Robert and David and their girlfriends, my mum and dad, Kate's mum and dad, her brother Andrew and his wife Sue, and Kate's friends Tom and Fiona Harrison; and my brothers Ian and David and their wives.

My brother Ian was my best man. Ian is 11 years younger than me and more like me than my two other brothers Andrew and David, who both joined the RAF and live in Germany and Luxembourg respectively. They've both done well for themselves, have family and David ended up as a Wing Commander! Ian went into the RAF too, as a fireman. He is very happily married to Ann and having helped me on my milk round, has had his own for many years.

Ian and I used to play golf every Thursday. I took up golf with him when I was working with Laycock's in the 90s. We'd play twice a week with the other round on a weekend. I was never a natural golfer, Ian was more natural than me, but I got to the stage where I could go round in 90 and got my handicap down to 18. We played at Shiptonthorpe and at Skelton and we joined Easingwold for a time. Funny really, when I played cricket and golf I played left-handed and yet I'm right-handed generally.

I mention the golf because Aldwark Manor has its own very good golf course and the plan was to play a round on the morning of the wedding, but that didn't materialise. I was the only one up in time. It was about 6 o'clock in the morning. England were playing one of the pool matches in the Rugby Wold Cup being held in New Zealand that morning.

The hotel grounds were bathed in beautiful early autumn morning sunshine. It was so fresh and so was I. As I was walking along in the gardens I saw one of the windows open and Ian put his head out for air. He looked like death warmed up, he was a bit worse for wear from the night before when there had been a rather unsuccessful attempt to get me absolutely blotto from my good friend and business associate Grant Webster, along with one or two others including Ian and David.

Grant is another representative who I have known in various guises since joining Laycock's. He is a fiery Scotsman, from Pitlochry, with a wicked sense of humour and enjoys a wee dram or two along with an immense amount of fun. He and his then boss Nick Burford played a trick on me many years ago at a Christmas party. This involved Nick pretending to be an Indian calling me on my mobile with hilarious results. They have both become great friends.

But any attempt at getting me drunk were to no avail.

I'd been very good, very strict – just like Farmer Chris – and had been in bed in my luxurious room all to myself by 9 o'clock as I was determined not to ruin Kate's and my big day. I looked up to Ian and said, 'You look bloody awful! You need to get yourself sorted out pal!'

We had a lovely wedding breakfast and were married by the registrar at 2 o'clock in the afternoon with many good friends attending including Richard and Fran Newby, Graham and Pauline Jewitt, Andrew and Christine Osguthorpe, all of whom remain great friends to us both.

The setting was just beautiful. We had a string trio playing. The atmosphere was exactly right. It was such a lovely day. The speeches went well with Ian and I having a little go at each other in the best of ways. When Ian was about to speak I said, 'Sadly my brother does suffer from a mental problem, so please don't listen to what he says as it is all wrong.'

There were somewhere around 150 at the evening 'do' where we had a disco and our first dance was to Jim Reeves' 'I Love You Because'. This was a great favourite of my dad's, who was still with us in 2011, and all of the family, we played it at his funeral, and it will be my final song at my funeral, although hopefully not for a while!

Kate and I often have music playing at home and especially in summer, as we live as much as possible outside and often barbecue our tea (dinner to you Southern softies!), and we both love the songs of Meat Loaf playing them in summer evenings at Spring View Farm. We recently saw the musical *Bat Out of Hell* in London. Kate's favourite song is 'Paradise by the Dashboard Light' and we had that as one of our songs at the wedding.

The following morning we were on a plane to Mallorca for our honeymoon where we stayed a week in a luxurious private villa with our own pool in Puerto Soller. Just the two of us.

Kate is the loveliest person anyone could wish for, there is simply not a bad bone in her body. She is the most wonderful wife in every way – even surpassing the previous two Mrs Jefferys with her cooking skills!

We often joke that she is 'Mrs J the Third' but all in good heart. Kate is so quiet and hates the limelight but knows how much I need her support with my new media career and I shall be forever grateful that she said yes to marrying me. We have never fallen out and never have a bad word for each other. We have worked side by side nearly every working day since 1997 and I absolutely couldn't have achieved any of what we have without her by my side.

CHAPTER 25

Let's Go Racing

Richard and Janet Taylor lived just up the road from us in Husthwaite and ran their own steel fabrication business. They are two of the kindest people you could imagine. Since meeting them in the pub in Husthwaite all those years ago they have become our closest friends and we have spent many a lovely day and evening in their company.

Their son Andy and his wife Helen have recently moved back to England from Helen's native Australia with their children Macie and Cohen. This has made Richard and Janet's life a lot easier as they used to spend a lot of time travelling Down Under. Andy now works in the business with them and they have a lovely house in Crayke.

I remember one of the first times we talked together as a four in the pub one night. I was in awe of Richard – and it wasn't just the Range Rover he drives or the Mercedes Sport that Janet has. I asked how many people they had working for them and Richard said, 'About half of them.' We hit it off from that point. Richard and Janet had a share in three racehorses.

Thirsk Races had approached us, as a local business, to advertise in their racecard and we liked the idea. When we asked about sponsorship we were told of the various options. The package we went for was to sponsor the leading jockey and leading trainer at Thirsk and that gave us free entry badges for the year, we were invited to the directors' box at the opening meeting of the year and had an advertisement in the racecard for the year. We went to every meeting and thoroughly enjoyed ourselves.

My brother Ian has some kind of weird system for backing horses that works, so we'd get there, I'd get a beer and ring him asking what he'd got for me. We would always come home up on the day in terms of our gambling, plus we'd had a few drinks, met a few people and had a great time.

The thrill of the races is fantastic, whether it is a daytime or night-time meeting. Kate has always had horses and rides out every day at home. We became caught up in the atmosphere and I said to Kate that I'd like to buy a share in a racehorse, like Richard and Janet.

I thought it would be nice to go with a local trainer. I spoke to a customer who knew I had an interest in racing and he recommended his relation Ruth Carr of Mowbray House in Stillington, who had taken out her trainer's licence in 2008, following her grandfather David Chapman who had retired that year and was a well-known racehorse trainer. He'd trained Chaplin's Club, Soba, Quito, Paddywack and loads of others who had all won lots of races.

We went to see Ruth, who has done everything in racing as a jockey and now a trainer. We met Ruth and her grandma Marion, David's widow, and they showed us around the stables. We had seen two we quite fancied – one a chestnut gelding and the other a grey. Kate loves greys.

As we sat in Ruth's conservatory this horse called Chosen One came up to the fence, put his head over and Ruth said, 'There's your horse.'

Chosen One was a chestnut gelding and he'd won a handful of races already in his early days. We paid for a quarter share along with a lady called Bridget Houlston who also had a quarter share. Ruth and Marion also had a quarter each, so we owned a leg apiece.

One of the most wonderful experiences is going to see

your own horse run. It makes the hairs on the back of your neck stand up when your horse comes on to the course ready to race, but the first year we had him in 2011 was a bit frustrating. He had a second at Pontefract and a third at Musselburgh. We were spending quite a bit of money on Colin, that was his stable name, and the idea was that he would hopefully win us some money.

I'd wanted a 5-furlong sprinter. To me that was really exciting. Each race takes less than a minute. Everything has to go right on the day to win – and he had a good track record having won previously to our ownership at Musselburgh, Beverley and Haydock Park, but 2011 wasn't his year, although he had come close.

25 May 2012 was to be a momentous day in Mr & Mrs Jeffery's racehorse ownership history. We were at Catterick. It was a lovely summer's evening. Chosen One/ Colin loved fast going. Ruth always has her horses turned out so well and when he came into pre-parade his coat was shining and he looked a picture with his big, powerful back end a sprinter needs.

We're now in the saddling enclosure, always an exciting part if you're an owner, because you get to be up close and personal with your horse. I wanted him to feel good and I wanted to help play my part. I would always hold him while they got his saddle on. I'd stroke him, pat him, talk to him like I did all those years ago with Grandad's Shires. It's really good to offer that personal touch and I really thought a lot of this horse, even if he'd not produced that win for us just yet.

Next, you're in the parade ring with your horse, with the other owners and trainers so that all the punters can see them, analyse them, check out how they are moving, reacting. This particular day he just looked absolutely stunning. It was an apprentice race and we had Shirley Teasdale on board. You get to talk with the jockey about what their tactics are going to be, then the bell rings, your heart starts pumping a bit and the announcement comes for all jockeys to mount. At that point all you have left is, 'Good luck, do your best,' and off they go.

When we first started as owners I thought the horses were going to be knackered by running all the way down to the start, but what did I know? By running to the start it helps them warm up.

I just had a good feeling about this race. It was a lovely evening. The ground was good; and we had a good draw. At Catterick you really need to be drawn on the inside to have the best chance of winning and we were in stall No 1.

We'd been a year with this bloody horse, which was another way of looking at things, but hadn't had a win – not that any horse has a divine right to win. It wasn't so much the money, although you can't forever do something that doesn't show some kind of return unless you're very rich, it was more about the excitement. I just wanted that adrenaline rush, that kick of cheering on a winner – our winner!

We had the going. We had the draw. I'm hoping Colin is going into the stalls last because he hates the stalls. He was last into the stalls.

I used to get so nervous and the only thing I could never understand was how a usually normal, sane, level-headed person can turn into some kind of gibbering, halfwit wreck when their horse is running, especially if it looks like it might win. You turn into something ridiculously abnormal, or I did!

And they're off!

Oh My God, here we go. Kate and I have taken up position at the finish line. Has he broke okay? Has he got out quick! He HAS got out quick!! My God he's broke well. He HAS broke well. He's looking good. He's looking really good. He's look ... Come on Colin! Come on Colin!

I'm jumping up and down. Colin's well into his stride, running like his hooves almost never touched the turf. He's running so smoothly and little Shirley Teasdale, this tiny little thing on his back who's never ridden him before, comes around the bend into sight, and ... He's in the lead!! He's in the lead!!! ... Come on Colin ... Come on Colin ... Come on COLLLLLLLLLLIN!!!!!!

And everybody around me is thinking who the f*** is Colin?!!

He's won! He's won! My God he's won! I was hugging people I'd never met before in my life, shaking people's hands. Our horse had won. Okay, it was Catterick in the evening, not Cheltenham Festival or Ladies Day at Ascot, but he'd won – by about 3 lengths.

We got out on to the course, myself and Bridget, and led him into the winner's enclosure. The Winner's Enclosure! We'd made it! And I will never forget just how much Colin was panting, really panting. This fantastic specimen of a gelding had just powered his way through 5 furlongs in about 58 seconds. I congratulated Shirley, patted Colin, and Ruth got him some water, gave him a drink, got his saddle off, walked him around and he was fine. More than fine. We'd WON!!

Even with all of that explanation it doesn't convey just how emotionally happy and excited I was that our horse had won. I could have cried with happiness. It meant so much and was just the most wonderful feeling. We received a trophy, had champagne, got a DVD of the race to relive it all again, but that minute, less than a minute – WOW!

Two months later, at Pontefract, he won again, and the following year won four times – twice at Catterick and once at Bath, and Pontefract again this time with his biggest win in the Chaplin's Club Handicap. He won it by half a length with Jimmy Sullivan riding him.

We had three wonderful years with Colin. We went to places I'd never been before – Musselburgh, Ayr, Hamilton, Bath and lots of local courses. He won 7 times for us with his last win at Ayr in July 2014. We had a great night going up there and seeing him win. The social side of racing is really good and if you are part of a syndicate you don't have to be wealthy to be a racehorse owner.

It ended up that he hadn't really cost us much or anything, that bit wasn't so important. I always put something on him to win too, not a lot, usually only around 20 quid, although I did have a go at £100 once. Colin's last race was at Redcar in October 2014 where he finished last. That's when Ruth said she thought he'd had enough and retired him. He's still alive now and we have popped in to see him since.

Ruth is a very amenable trainer, she looks after her horses, her people and her owners. I wish we had the time to do it all again, but the way things are currently with the business, the farm and the TV stuff, we just don't have the time, but back then we'd think nothing of driving three and a half hours to an evening meeting at Musselburgh to see Colin run for less than a minute!

For anyone remotely interested in horse racing, a trip to Newmarket, the 'home of racing', is a must. This is where to see the top trainers with the very best racehorses in the world. The gallops are a must, especially early morning, to see these wonderful animals put through their paces.

Kate and I had the good fortune of being invited to Banstead Manor Stud, the Newmarket home of Juddmonte Farms. There was a rather famous stallion we were extremely excited to meet.

One of our customers back in Thirsk was the manager of Cliffe Stud just outside Helmsley, part of the Sir Henry Cecil operation. Guy knew we liked our racing and I mentioned one day how much I would love to visit

Banstead Manor and see Frankel.

'Leave it with me,' he said. The next week we had our invites and planned to go when the famous Cambridgeshire meeting is held at the Rowley Mile course.

I spoke to Ruth and asked if she could get us badges for the meeting. 'I can do better than that,' she said. 'I have a horse running at the meeting and you can have owners' and trainers' badges!' This was wonderful news. These badges give you access to the best facilities and lunch, access to the parade ring and enclosures.

We set off for our date with Frankel!

Banstead Manor is quite amazing. Owned by Prince Khalid Abdulla it epitomises the sport of kings in every way possible. Huge entrance gates securely locked were opened for us by a guard. I remember thinking about when Shergar was stolen. The value of horses here runs into hundreds of millions of pounds! No wonder the security was so tight.

We were invited into the trophy room where we could see Frankel's trophies and of course the famous Juddmonte turquoise and pink silks that he carried when racing. We felt immensely privileged. The stud manager then took us to the stables that

were all individually built and offered every comfort with a padded floor and walls to prevent injuries. They were also rather large, like a small bungalow!

Our hearts started to beat a bit quicker as we saw a horse being led towards us out of a stable. The man leading the horse was immaculately dressed and the horse looked incredible too with a sleek shiny coat.

This was Oasis Dream. We were told all about his breeding and history, then another one arrived, Dansili, just as stunning, another very famous stallion. But then, here he came. The most famous racehorse in the world. Frankel.

He was led to the front and we stood next to him, stroked him and had photos taken with him. He wasn't as tall as I'd expected, even though I'd seen him run at York. I asked if Kate, as an experienced horse woman, could sit on him but this was politely declined! He was so chilled and relaxed and looked amazing.

We were told he covered up to 4 mares a day in the season. Yes, 4 a day! His fee? £125,000 per cover. I have since learnt this has now increased to £175,000 per cover. Wow! And he has many years of good service to come.

It all ended too quickly, but we had an amazing couple of hours looking round the stud, the trophies and of course the horses. I thought back to the day we saw Frankel win the Juddmonte race at York's Ebor meeting.

I have never ever witnessed such passion and love for a racehorse as I did that day. There were thousands dressed in his colours and waving flags. We had a great position on the finish line and watched as he came around the left-hand bend into the final few furlongs. Tom Quealley, his jockey, let him go and he won so easily sending thousands of people into ecstasy. I had put a tenner on him to win but I didn't cash it. I got Tom Quealley to sign it and have kept it safe at home.

We stayed overnight in Bury St Edmunds and then travelled to Newmarket racecourse on Saturday morning for a day at the Rowley Mile course with our O&T badges. The Cambridgeshire meeting's top race of the day had a prize of over £100,000 to the winner. A mere drop in the ocean I thought compared to what Frankel has earned today!

Kate and I like to see the horses close up and spent much time around the parade ring and near the course itself. We didn't win much, as I recall, but I will be forever grateful to Ruth for getting the badges and providing us with a very nice day and making it a very special 'Frankel' weekend.

Our passion for horse racing even saw Kate and I receive an invitation from Chanelle McCoy, wife of Sir AP McCoy, and owner of a pharmaceutical company at the time, to the first day of the Cheltenham Gold Cup meeting where we experienced and were part of the Cheltenham Roar – from our private box with HRH Princess Anne and Zara next to us in the Royal Box!

CHAPTER 26

Barra

Television has become an important part of my life recently with appearances on *The Yorkshire Vet* and of course *Celebs on the Farm*. I have such fond memories of television programmes when I was growing up. *Morecambe and Wise, On The Buses, Fawlty Towers, The Good Life* and *Dad's Army*. All warm and funny shows.

It was a part of family life as we all gathered together to watch. We had no means of recording and 'catch up' wasn't heard of! *Dad's Army* was and still is my absolute favourite. I never get sick of watching it and if I've had a long day it's a real treat to watch an episode of this endearing show.

One of my favourite characters is Private Frazer, played by John Laurie, the tight Scotsman who rolled his eyes and often referred back to his childhood and spoke of 'a wild and lonely place, the isle of Barra.' Only a few years ago, after discovering Google, I decided to see if Barra was a fictional place or if it actually existed. What I found amazed me. After viewing Barra from the wonders of Google Earth I decided I simply had to go! I told Kate of my plans. She thought I was mad, but agreed, and we booked a cottage on the island.

In September 2012 we set off in the pickup with both our dogs on board and made for Oban, booked on the ferry. It was a Sunday. Not bad for traffic and driving north is so much more pleasurable than going south! The roads are quieter and the scenery just gets better the further north you go. We stopped at the motorway services at Carlisle for breakfast, then Loch Lomond for lunch (Kate loves making a picnic).

Oban really is lovely and ferries sail to all the Hebridean islands. We were bound for Castlebay on Barra sailing at 3pm and arriving 5 hours later after 90 miles of sea.

We were surprised at the size of the ferry. They are operated by Caledonian MacBrayne, commonly known as Calmac. We made sure the dogs were comfortable in the back of the pickup and went upstairs. Jack Russells wouldn't settle in the main deck.

Neither of us had been to the Outer Hebrides. This was another adventure! The ferry has a bar, café and lounges, but we decided to go up on the outside top deck to say goodbye to Oban.

It was freezing! Blowing a gale and raining. We didn't say goodbye for long! The first hour or so of the journey is very calm passing the Isle of Mull, before reaching the open waters of the Atlantic. Then you really know that you are on a ship!

It was getting dark as we approached Barra. We drove off and it was pouring down, pitch black! Private Frazer's words were true. 'A wild and lonely place!'

There is only one road on Barra, which basically takes you round the island with smaller roads off it to the various beaches and houses. We were heading to North Bay at the other side of the island.

The road is single track with passing places. It was now 9.30pm, dark and raining hard. Where had we come to?

Fortunately, after we'd been driving for about 15 minutes and using Google Maps we came to the junction where I knew we needed to turn left, and the owner of the cottage was there flashing the cottage lights on and off to let us know where to go! He had the fire lit and the place was warm and very suitable for our stay. We'd made it from Thornton on the Hill to our 'wild and lonely place' on Barra! We had left home at 7 that morning and it was now 10 at night.

The next morning was lovely with blue skies and sunshine, a stiff breeze but about 12 degrees and really pleasant. We had brought our own bacon and eggs from the farm and enjoyed a lovely cooked breakfast before going off to explore.

North Bay is on the way to the island's airport where the planes, two per day from Glasgow, land on the beach. Exactly where they land and take off depends on the weather and the tide! We set off to see for ourselves, flask and sandwiches packed, and the dogs enjoying themselves. About two miles from our cottage we found it, after taking in the most glorious hillside that looks over the huge bay with miles and miles of white sand. This is Traigh Mhor, Barra's famous cockle beach, where every morning the local shellfish men are there harvesting cockles in the old-fashioned way by hand.

We parked on the machair, which are grassy dunes. The airport was at rush hour with at least 8 people sat in the café area! It's actually a café with an airport attached! Check-in was open, which is literally the size of a small front room. We heard the noise of propellers and a twin-engined Otter aircraft appeared taxiing up the beach and stopping right outside the window!

This is a lifeblood for Barra. The planes carry up to 18 and are operated by Loganair. They can take off and land in the most awful conditions. What a wonderful way to arrive we thought. Apparently this is the only airport in the world where there are scheduled landings on a beach. Watching the plane take off from the beach was amazing.

Discovering new beaches, new walks and the delights of the two pubs on the island formed our time on Barra, along with a return to this wholly unique airport.

One of our favourite places to stop for a drink anywhere

in the world is now the decking at the front of the Craigard Hotel in Castlebay. Here you can look out over the bay with its famous medieval Kisimul castle on its own island and the island of Vatersay beyond. On a clear day you can see the uninhabited islands of Pabay, Sandray and Mingerlay. Truly spectacular views.

The island of Barra is about 8 miles long by 4 wide so it's impossible to get lost and everyone is so friendly. Even the drivers! Since going there Kate and I always say that if someone coming towards us in a vehicle doesn't give way, they should be sent to Barra to learn road courtesy! Everyone gives way to the other vehicle, it's a real pleasure.

The island of Vatersay is attached to Barra via a causeway. Here there are some lovely walks and some cattle too, as it is more grassy than Barra. We discovered the most pristine beaches here with pure white sand lapped by the clearest turquoise sea. It really looks like the Caribbean in places apart from the temperature difference! The cattle here have their own beaches and many a time you will stumble across a small beach with cows and calves laid on it as though they are on holiday.

There are ferries running to the island of Eriskay every hour or so from Barra. Once on Eriskay it is possible to drive up through South Uist, Benbecula and North Uist then Bernaray and then take another ferry up to Harris and Lewis. Eriskay Bay is the scene of a famous shipwreck, the SS Politician which ran aground full of 28,000 cases of whisky, bound for Jamaica during the Second World War. The islanders had a good time salvaging this and although a real event, it was made into a film in 1949 called *Whisky Galore*, which was remade in 2016. The author of the film was Compton McKenzie and his house is still on the island near the airport.

Barra is the most special place for us, as we enjoy it due to its remoteness, peace and tranquillity. It is indeed

Farming, Celebs and Plum Pudding Pigs!

a wild place, as Private Frazer expounds, however not lonely with just over 1000 permanent inhabitants.

For us it was a week without telephones or computers, just basic living in an old-fashioned cottage and exploring the stunning coastline, beaches and hills, eating fantastic sea food and drinking Guinness! Castlebay the main settlement is lovely and has a school, a hotel, a pub and a few shops.

One very sad and poignant memory however is of a young girl who died in the Manchester bombings in 2017. She was only 16 and from Vatersay. On our last visit to Vatersay, more recently, we went to her grave to pay our respects. It is in the settlement of Caolas, which is the westernmost permanently inhabited place in Great Britain. She is laid to rest in a very simple graveyard on the machair, overlooked by hills and next to the sea, it was a peaceful but extremely sad occasion as we felt an affinity toward this family having made several visits to Vatersay since our first in 2012.

It's hard to believe that this remote part of the world could be affected by the tragic events of that awful day.

We have also been lucky enough to travel to the archipelago of St Kilda. This group of islands is another 40 miles west of North Uist in the Atlantic and we booked a trip from Harris. St Kilda was inhabited until 1930 but there's only a small number of MOD people there now. It's a world heritage site and there is work going on to restore some of the original houses.

The neighbouring isles of Boreray and Soay are home to the indigenous populations of sheep of the same name. The seas are full of wildlife and we saw minke whales, dolphins, seals, thousands of gannets and puffins. A truly magical place as is the whole of the Outer Hebrides.

They truly are 'The islands on the edge of the world' and a very special place for Farmer Chris and Mrs J the Third!

CHAPTER 27

Let's Go Farming

When Kate and I started out on our own in 2004, taking over Ray Green's business, I had wonderful ambitions. I was 46 and when you're that age you've a lot of energy and stamina. I could see the massive potential of the sector we were in, all we had to do was exactly what we were doing, which was simply giving fantastic service to people with a great range of products at a competitive price and keep adding to our range. I wanted to take over the world.

I knew that Kate was the good person at my side to do that – and that I was the aggressive marketeer, and that got me into some business fights and problems.

The established big boys in our area and market sector were Farmway, the agricultural co-operative. I'd already had altercations with them over the sale of Ray Green's business to us in 2004 and our move to the new Thirsk livestock market and rural centre in 2006.

When we really started building our trade the Farmway people thought they could easily put us out of business by cutting their prices, undercutting us.

I struck lucky by meeting this man called Francis O'Farrell in Northern Ireland and found he could supply a lot of the animal medicines we stocked at a much more competitive price than I had ever realised. Francis loved that we were the underdogs and he supported us. I bought a lot of products through him that I was able to put out at less than Farmway could – and I was still making a margin.

There was one occasion when my aggression cost

me an apology and a payment to Farmway. I'd written something that was published in the press about how good the service was that we give at Green's and how an independent store was superior to some of the larger businesses in the area. I may have been a little more vitriolic about it at the time too! Basically, I had indicated that we were far superior and Farmway, although not mentioned by name, shouldn't be trusted.

Farmway took me to task over this. I received a solicitor's letter from them threatening a libel case and my solicitor took one look at the offending article before telling me I had to pay them off. If it went to court he reckoned it would cost me £20,000, but I could risk it if I'd like to!

I wrote a letter of apology and paid them an agreed settlement, but there's more than one way to skin a cat and that's when I really did ram home our superior service. I became even more aggressive in my marketing and was even more determined to get more business from them. Nobody wants to see a farmer cooperative or any business go, but to my mind from what I saw at the time, it really was run very poorly.

The worst thing they could have done was to take me to task over that article. It made my resolve even stronger, like a red rag to a bull. I worked smarter – and harder than ever. I made sure I got back at those who appeared to be waging a personal vendetta against me. I never stopped. We were at every sale, every venue, every event, we were direct marketing, we were advertising in newspapers and then on social media, we rang people, grabbed people in the market and we matched anything they could come up with – and our stores became the place to be.

By 2011 we had the main store at Thirsk, we had moved out of the bothy at Northallerton for larger premises on an industrial estate and we had a Portakabin store at Ruswarp livestock market near Whitby. We took on a small unit at Wharfedale Farmers Market in Otley for 6 months but it wasn't worth it and we'd continued with Malton livestock market for a short while after Judy had left around 2008. We had a very likeable young man called Richard Thompson at Ruswarp who was well known in the area and he grew the business really well.

As much as I was motivated to do well with Green's and looking after farmers, I still had that desire to farm too.

Kate and I were happy where we lived in Husthwaite, but I still hankered after having a farm and both of us are really farming people. We started looking around for a smallholding in 2013. After we'd been to see several places a bit further away from our local area my mind kept coming back to the TV programmes we'd watched where there was a big compromise that people couldn't make when thinking of moving and we realised we were the same.

We knew we then had to find something in our area. Kate knew of this place that was called Yeoman's Barn and had been on the market for a year and a half. I'd never been here, to Thornton on the Hill, but Kate used to ride her horse Cloudy out this way. She had Cloudy stabled opposite Wortley Cottage at the time.

When we first saw what was Yeoman's Barn that is now Spring View Farm it looked a dump. My first thought was there was no way I wanted us to buy it. Overgrown, dreadful looking. It was terrible, no way, that was that.

The chap that owned it sold wood and logs. We had a log burner and he brought logs to us at Husthwaite. We got talking and he mentioned about taking a look at his place. I didn't like to say that I already had and had discounted it.

We saw him again one afternoon in the pub in

Husthwaite and, clearly keen on netting us as a buyer, he asked when we were going to take a look. I'd only driven by previously. We weren't doing much that day, so we went back with him and took a proper look.

Within about 20 minutes I said to Kate, 'I want us to buy this place.' I found the potential of it was invigorating, the excitement of taking it on immense. It was a bit like when I went to work with Laycock's in Malton and when we took on Green's. I set foot on the land and in the house, which was exactly the wreck I'd originally seen, and thought what fun we would have sorting out the mess, renovating and making something really special. Kate couldn't believe what I was saying after what I'd said originally.

Could we afford the asking price? No. Big problem. We had to do two things. Agree a lower price and find a way of buying it – and where there's a will, there is a way. The vendor was desperate to sell as he wanted to travel the world. We agreed a lower price.

We sold Wortley Cottage, which gave us a deposit towards the figure we needed and we had other monies between us, but we couldn't afford the whole thing that included the house, gardens and 10 acres with a range of farm buildings.

We went to our bank manager at HSBC. They have always been supportive of everything we have done at Green's and she solved our shortage of funds by telling us we could put what we needed for the land and buildings down as a commercial mortgage on the basis that our Green's business clearly needs storage.

Moving house is always stressful, but when you take into account the splitting of title deeds, dealing with the Land Registry, dealing with a vendor at one end who just wants it sorting so that he can move on and a buyer of our property at another that wanted to move in or would pull out of the sale, it was a nightmare.

We ended up moving out of Wortley Cottage to save the sale, putting our furniture into storage at work and moving into a cottage for six weeks that our friends Tim and Ann Robson let us have for nothing. So good of them.

Eventually everything was agreed and we moved here to what was then still Yeoman's Barn on 2 November 2015. I hated the name. Its original name, as we found on old Ordnance Survey maps had been Spring View Farm, so we wrote to the council to have its name changed back. The main thing though was we were here. I was ecstatic. I had a farm. We had our own farm.

CHAPTER 28

Let's Go and Buy Some Sheep ... and Cattle ... and Pigs

I couldn't wait to buy some sheep, cattle and pigs, and get a tractor to start riving out dilapidated fencing and making things right. And I didn't. Wait, I mean. I didn't wait at all! By the time we arrived on the farm we already had 50 Mule ewes that had been here about 5 or 6 weeks before the sale was officially completed – and two rare, pedigree Whitebred Shorthorn cattle were being carefully looked after by their original owners in readiness for them to arrive at Spring View Farm just after we had moved in. Excited doesn't do justice to how I felt at the time.

It was fantastic! I was like a pig in the proverbial! I was out mixing milk, feeding calves, mucking out pigs and looking with love in my eyes at my cows thinking how wonderful it was having these beautiful pedigree Whitebred Shorthorns and my favourite plum pudding pigs, the Oxford Sandy & Blacks. I was really passionate about having animals and felt it would give us something that would hopefully turn into income the following year. I can feel some of my farmer customers and friends smiling at my naivety, but nothing was going to stop me and in no time at all this place was alive with the sounds of sheep, cattle and pigs!

We had started buying livestock at the Great Yorkshire Show in July 2015, four months before we arrived at Spring View Farm and with no absolute guarantee that everything would go through! We hadn't planned on buying anything, honestly we hadn't!

The Great Yorkshire Show is our county's and one of the country's biggest agricultural shows and is a fabulous three-day event. We'd always been interested in rare breeds and particularly enjoy seeing them at the show and other shows. I've always been a pig man at heart and had always fancied having some Oxford Sandy & Blacks that are known as 'plum pudding pigs' and we saw some at the show.

But love was to call when we went into the Rare Breeds Survival Trust (RBST) stand and marquee and I saw the Whitebred Shorthorn cow Elizabeth and her calf. We met their owner Helen Marginson from Burnley in Lancashire and that's how it became our most expensive Great Yorkshire Show ever! We asked to visit Helen's farm and bought two Whitebred Shorthorn cows – Bertha and Lockie.

Helen then agreed to keep them until our move to Spring View was completed.

Anna (Butler) who has worked with us for over 14 years, and farms at Great Ayton, sold us 50 Mule ewes. We borrowed two tups from customers – a Texel and a Suffolk – with a view to producing butchers' lambs. I joke now that we bought these so that they would give Kate 'something to do' in the spring, as well as it being one of the busiest times of the year for us at Green's! I can see Kate rolling her eyes at me now.

Pigs were next to arrive. We'd been at Spring View two days when I bought 10 Berkshire X pigs! Calves were next. I'd become a big fan of the online site www.sellmylivestock.co.uk and over a period starting as soon as we landed at the farm I began buying calves that we bucket-reared. I also bought some calves from local farmers too. I was buying anything I could as I was now Farmer Chris – and I was definitely going to be Farmer Chris from now on!

We had a real mixed bag of calves by the time I stopped buying. Aberdeen Angus X, Jersey X, Belgian Blue X – you name it, I'd bought it. I had a lot of shed space to fill and I was determined to fill it. They were arriving from everywhere with the idea they would be ready for turnout in May – and the lambs, of which we had 75, were born in March. It was mayhem!

I also decided it would be nice to have a donkey. So I found a lady who had one to sell, locally, but she said I would have to take its foal too. While I was there buying this donkey, and now its foal, these cute little pigmy goats appeared. I came home with two donkeys, three pregnant pigmy goats and a billy. Kate wasn't amused but saw the funny side. I was gathering a real menagerie (always think of Cockney Rebel when I use that word) and I was loving it!

Here's what Kate says about that time: 'Chris was rampaging around saying 'I'll have to have calves, have to have pigs, have to have sheep, that's just how he is. It's lucky the calves had me looking after them as Chris was just all over the place. Chris has this little saying, 'I want'. It was rather chaotic.'

I needed a tractor. I started riving out the old fencing and clearing all the rubbish. The grass was terrible, that needed sorting. Tim (Robson), who'd let Kate and I stay in the cottage for the time in between us selling at Husthwaite and being able to move in at the farm, is also a tractor dealer and just told me to take this Deutz Fahr tractor and see how it went. I paid him for it months later. I set to work on the fencing, the garden, making everything right and over quite a period of the next few years, with the help of local landscaper Mark Hopkins who laid the lawn in the garden, and fencing contractor Will Gray, it is all now in pretty good shape.

Elsie arrived in 2015, our Oxford Sandy & Black gilt.

By springtime we had growing calves, loads of them; ewes lambing; the Whitebred Shorthorns gave us two bull calves; we had Elsie to get in-pig; I'm riving out bushes, trees, anything that needed to go; we're pulling off old wallpaper, pulling out staircases, generally ripping the house and garden area apart; we've animals everywhere! And I've got a smile on my face about a mile long because I'm loving it.

Green's had paid for everything at the time, which Kate wasn't happy about but begrudgingly agreed. She looks after the purse strings, which is just as well, but things were starting to get a little tight, business was already proving more difficult at that time without adding the purchase of livestock, tractors and fencing into the mix.

I also quickly learned that you don't make money out of buying a rag, tag and bobtail load of calves and 50 Mule ewes, because the money just isn't there. All we were doing was working harder, adding to our already busy workload with our massive renovation and clean-up project and life at Green's all being full-on. It wasn't until a few years later that Kate and I began restructuring our business at Green's too.

We had fallen into rare breeds through buying the Whitebreds and it took me two or three years to realise they were potentially one form of livestock that could make us anything. They are so rare, and we love having them. We're now firmly embedded in a breeding programme growing the herd and selling to other breeders. We have done the same with Oxford Sandy & Blacks and have also been in and out of Kerry Hill sheep (Stephen Bailey, eat your heart out!).

Those first two Whitebred Shorthorn bull calves gave us so much fun. We showed one of them – Springview Roxburgh at Cleveland County Show and Ryedale Show, picking up a championship in the Native Cattle Any Other

Breed class. We took him to the spring breed sale at Carlisle in 2017.

I remember being so nervous taking him into the ring because I was now showing him to sell, against others from the breed. This is where it counts. We didn't sell him that spring, but we showed him again in the autumn sale and he came third in his bull class.

Kate had done the most amazing job of combing him up and preparing him. I'd walked him around the ring while the bidding took place. We'd decided we would sell him if he made 2000 guineas, you put down a reserve price that unless it reaches you will withdraw and take your beast home. I thought the bidding had stopped at 1800, but it didn't. We sold him for 2400 guineas! He was the highest priced bull of the day!

That's when the penny dropped! It was a bit like my Colin moment! I was almost a gibbering wreck again. We'd sold a beast we had reared for 2400 guineas! That same day we also saw this most beautiful heifer make 5000 guineas. My jaw dropped. This was something we could do. We'd found a way that I could see our little farm could work, by concentrating on rare breeds.

CHAPTER 29

The Yorkshire Vet

We have a farm. We have animals. We need a vet. We were registered with Skeldale Vets, the famous veterinary centre where author James Herriot / vet Alf Wight wrote his books that brought about the films and TV series *All Creatures Great & Small.*

These days one of the most watched TV programmes on Channel 5, pulling in over 2 million viewers, is *The Yorkshire Vet* featuring Julian Norton. We'd had a visit from a lady vet previously and then Julian came to see one of our cows. We'd met with Julian and his now former colleague Peter Wright about six months earlier to see whether Skeldale and Green's could work together, so Julian and I knew each other a little.

Our first story on *The Yorkshire Vet* was about Kate's horse Cloudy who had scratched his eye, but that was while we were still at Wortley Cottage. We now had a farm and a beautiful setting. We'd been at Spring View around six months when Julian arrived with his two-woman TV crew of Laura and LJ. He'd asked if I minded them filming what he was doing with the cow, with me around as he was explaining what he was doing.

This was my first time being involved with any kind of filming. I soon got to understand that if you're involved in TV work you cannot mind being messed around a little bit and how long it takes just to make sure of even a one-minute piece. You have to spend a lot of time so that they can capture what they want or what happens when you least expect it!

Series 2 –
The Celebs
gather in
the barn on
the first day

Me and
Stephen –
the dream
team back
together!

Photoshoot for title pics for *Celebs on the Farm* Series 2

Charlie Edwards v Big Farmer Chris – World Title Fight

Playing football with a legend – and my second *Celebs on the Farm* Champion – Paul Merson

Crissy almost became my on-screen wife!

The gorgeous Caprice

Me and the kids!

The lovely David Potts

Contemplation before making my final decision

Series 2 – The Final 4

Series 3 – The Celebs back in the barn!

Meet my new farming son Stephen, finally dressing the part!

The Celebs
find out their
accommodation

Farmer Chris –
The Cameraman

Mr Duncan James from pop group Blue, modelling my truck

Fast Lad! Not me, 100 metres champion Harry Aikines-Aryeetey

Linda Robson, lovely lady

Cheryl Hole, interesting lady!

Kerry Katona, gorgeous lady

The GooWoo production team that make *Celebs on the Farm*

'Have you seen who's in this book?'
The kids like it!

Celebs & Alpacas, a curious mix

That's make-up everybody, I didn't fall! Photoshoot Day!

My own logo!

Marley and Maisie helping Grandad at Spring View Farm!

Grandson William in his new York City kit

Proud Grandad with baby Maddox our latest Jeffery boy!

Getting my kit off for a *Celebs on the Farm* calendar

I was enjoying my moment. Like a lot of people, I was excited that this might actually be on the telly and also discovered that a lot of people don't want to be filmed. I guess I'm just the sort of bloke who does like the idea. I liked the idea of publicity and thought it wouldn't do me any harm. It would be good for our customers and I'd be like them, as many of them have appeared too. I also thought that, to them, it would show me as a farmer instead of a man who runs a shop.

Julian, Laura and LJ all seemed to like filming here and I made them all a cuppa, we chatted more and Laura said that if there was anything I ever wanted to do that would make a good scene to let them know as they were always on the lookout for storylines for the show.

Elsie duly arrived in the spring that year in 2016 and I rang Julian to tell him that I had this beautiful rare breed, Oxford Sandy & Black plum pudding pig to artificially inseminate (known as AI in the farming world) to get her pregnant and would he and the crew like to come along and film it with Julian conducting the insemination. Spunky idea!

Julian thought it was marvellous and the TV crew would absolutely love it. What none of us knew at the time was just how much of a TV moment it would become.

The scene was set. I had the semen delivered on the Friday morning. The parcel arrived with two long catheters. Julian duly arrived at 2 o'clock as I'd rung to tell him she was on heat and ready. I had Elsie ready in her straw pen and a boar next to her. I didn't want the boar serving her because I wanted this best quality boar semen. I was on a mission in various ways, not just to provide a TV scene but also to prove to a few doubters that she wouldn't hold in pig.

The semen was ready. The catheter was ready. Julian was ready. The crew was here. And my starring role was to play the part of the boar pig!

I'm a pig man. Remember, this is where I started off in my working life, working with pigs. When you are inseminating a pig you sit on its back to ensure it is on heat and it stands, so I'm sitting on the pig pretending to be the boar. It's nothing unusual to me and in the pig trade it happens all the time.

This all turned into comedy. Julian gets behind Elsie in readiness to inseminate her. He takes the top off the bottle of semen – and he gets what is known in some forms of life as a facial! The semen spurted all over his face! The girls from the TV are laughing their boobs off! It was hilarious.

But there's a serious thing going on here. I want my sow pregnant to this quality boar's semen so that I can not only have some really good pigs, but also so that I can keep some of the progeny and grow my rare breed sow herd. While what has just happened really was funny, this is actually very important to me.

Julian's second attempt saw him get the catheter in successfully, so that it fitted into the cervix and when the whole scene was shown it was edited beautifully, they'd added funny music and it became one of the most watched episodes. And the really important thing farm wise was Elsie's pregnancy saw her produce 9 healthy pigs.

I think the production company at Daisybeck Studios in Leeds then saw that Julian and I have a natural way with each other, get on well and that what we are doing at Spring View Farm is a bit different, which is even more so now with our specialisation into rare breeds. It's also a very picturesque farm with nice animals. From that point on, any time Julian came here the crew came too.

I still have farmer customers come into our store at Thirsk who say, 'By 'eck lad, when you were riding that pig, what a laugh we 'ad!' They related to it and it worked for TV, for me and for Julian. I make no bones about it, I loved it and it gave me a taste for more.

Other scenes we've filmed for *The Yorkshire Vet* have included a boar needing its tusks removing; a heifer calving at 1 in the morning; a Highland cow having her horns taken off because she was stabbing the Whitebred Shorthorns; and a quite emotional scene for me, when my favourite cow Bertha, one of our original two Whitebred Shorthorns, had a cancerous growth on her bottom eyelid that led to taking her eye out. It was a horrible thing to have to do, but Julian, who had now moved to Ray Bean & Partners in Boroughbridge, had told me it was either that or have her killed.

Bertha was in-calf when we found out and Julian kept the cancer at bay until she calved in June 2019. When he operated on her he took out the whole eye and the top and bottom eyelids and stitched up what was left. There was no grafting. The place was like a bloodbath, like you'd imagine being in a slaughterhouse with buckets of blood everywhere. He was worried that the cancerous growth had gone a long way down. He cut it all out.

I was really quite worried a week later when where Bertha's eye had been was bulging almost as though she had a tennis ball under her skin, but Julian said it would fill with blood and she would gradually absorb it.

Two months later she and her calf were doing wonderfully well, as though nothing had ever happened. Bertha really is an incredible cow and all credit to Julian for taking on the task. She was 10 years old when he took it on. To give you an indication of why a cow like Bertha is worth saving, not just as an animal I love, she could have another five more calves and they could bring about a reasonable income. If the cancer had been on a different cow, with lesser breeding, then I probably wouldn't have been able to afford to do it. That's farming.

I had my first starring film role appearing in a promotional video for Green's where the producer had taken me for an outside shot on the top of our bloody hill on the coldest day imaginable that winter. I had been 600ft above sea level, with brain freeze, trying to remember the lines he had scripted. That man was the same man who has put together this book with me!

The out-takes from that promotional video are so funny, as I try, again and again, to get the lines right, but what we achieved was so good it really helped sell a product that we sell in our business called Lazer Tags.

Two years from my first experience of television I was to receive the opportunity I would never have imagined would come my way, but there was a lot to happen before then.

CHAPTER 30

Kate's Fall

It was a lovely Sunday morning 31 July 2016. I'd been up early and had called in at work. I'd come home to do some fencing. Anthony Harding Smith – 'Anth' – our painter and decorator had arrived to wallpaper our downstairs loo with some fancy 'duck' wallpaper costing £60 a roll. £60! I had told Kate, I wasn't prepared to touch it at that kind of money! Kate and I had a coffee and off she went for her horse ride, as she always did on a Sunday. I got the tractor and trailer ready and set off into the fields with my fencing equipment.

Kate's horse was a grey mare called Tilly, a flighty bloody thing. I never really got on with it, as it would try and bite me if I got too close! It was a lovely summer's day with blue sky, white fluffy clouds and a warm breeze. I had lost all track of time. I don't wear a watch but thought she'd been away a long time. I carried on with my jobs until all of a sudden I heard the clickety-clack of a helicopter. It was heading right for me really low and I realised it was the Air Ambulance, bright yellow.

Bloody hell, it swooped down just over me and went over the hill at the far end of my farm where I presumed it landed. I thought to myself, Christ, I hope it's not the missus. I carried on with my work again and about 20 minutes later I could hear someone shouting.

I looked up and it was Anth our decorator stood at the field gate. 'Chris, come quick, Kate's had an accident.' Jackie Barlow, a neighbour who has alpacas, had rung to say Kate had come off Tilly on Beacon Banks, the ridge running behind our farm and the ambulance was on its way.

Jackie came down the road with Tilly and told me in person: 'Kate's had a bad accident Chris, you need to come.' She put the horse into the paddock, removed its tack and took it into the shed. We both got into my pickup and drove to the village of Husthwaite where a track leads up to Beacon Banks which is a bridleway route and used by many horse riders and walkers.

Jackie didn't know what had happened, only that the helicopter had landed in her field and the horse was Kate's and needed catching. She knew Kate was injured badly but that was all. When we got there the road ambulance had arrived but couldn't get anywhere near the scene. There was a village first responder at the track end and he told me the Air Ambulance had taken Kate to hospital.

Which hospital? No-one knew. There were a few people gathered as word had quickly spread that someone had been injured. Will Mowatt lived opposite the entrance to the track. He had been to the scene and told me the ambulance was going to James Cook University Hospital in Middlesbrough. He said Kate was conscious but her arm was badly cut and she was complaining about abdominal pains.

I decided to go home and try to think what I had to do. As soon as I got home a lady arrived with Kate's riding hat, and whip. She told me to get a few things together and get to the hospital. I was in a daze. I simply couldn't think straight. I rang my good friend Tim Robson. Kate rides out with his wife Ann. He told me to stay at home and he would send Ann round straight away.

I started to get a bag ready for Kate. What do I put in it? I gathered a few toiletries and underwear. Then I thought, why am I getting a bag ready? I need to get to the bloody hospital! With that Ann arrived.

Farming, Celebs and Plum Pudding Pigs!

'What the fuck has happened?' Ann's language is always colourful. I told her I had to get to hospital. Kate had come off the horse. 'Right,' she said, 'get in the fucking car quick, you're in no fit state to drive. I'm taking you.' No-one messes with Ann in this mood.

We live in a fairly remote area and as we reached the village of Oulston there were signs up saying 'road closed – cycling event'. Ann took no notice of this and kept going. A race marshal flagged her down and stopped her saying she couldn't go through. This was not a sensible thing to say.

'Oh yes I fucking am, my friend has had a serious accident and I need to get to the hospital,' and with that she put her foot down and left the poor man bewildered and probably thinking he had never seen anyone that angry before!

It normally takes a good 45 minutes to get to James Cook Hospital, but we must have done it in 30. I couldn't believe how fast she drove. When we got there Ann pulled up right at the front entrance on double yellow lines with an adjacent sign saying, 'No parking, ambulance only'. I said, 'Ann, you can't park here.' She said, 'Oh yes I fucking can, come on!'

This was Sunday. The place was full of walking wounded from the remnants of what some imagine is a typical Saturday night out in 'Boro'. We approached the desk with Ann pushing past people who had been queuing up.

'Where is she?' Ann demanded. 'Kate Jeffery, she's come in with the Air Ambulance.' We were directed round the corner and into the day ward. Off we went. It was like being back with my mother! Ann leading the way and demanding to see Kate.

We arrived in the A&E ward behind the reception area with cubicles everywhere all with curtains round them. 'Can I help Madam?' a nurse said, looking at Ann as though she shouldn't be there. 'Kate Jeffery,' Ann said. 'Are you related, Madam?'

'Yes,' she said. 'I'm her best friend! Oh, and this is her husband!' I smiled weakly. 'Come with me,' she announced. We followed her toward a cubicle, she opened the curtain and there was Kate on a bed with a doctor and nurse in attendance.

They were trying to get a drip into her but couldn't get it in properly. Kate was still fully clothed, but her arm was bandaged and covered in blood. She was pleased to see us, but said her tummy was hurting.

The usual things were happening, blood pressure, temperature being taken, but Ann then made her presence felt again: 'You should go and get a doctor to put that drip in because you're making a mess of her arm.' With that a senior doctor arrived and we were asked to leave while they assessed her. I told Ann she should go and move her car before someone removed it. She decided that was a good idea.

I waited in reception until Ann came back after parking her car in the right area! It was only 10 minutes or so, but when we went back in to see Kate she'd been moved. The nurse told us she had gone to a pre-op assessment room, so we went there. My God! She was laid on the hospital trolley still fully clothed but now with so many instruments connected to her. This was a scary place to be for the faint-hearted and I was expecting the worst.

There were surgeons, doctors and nurses. Everyone was talking and some were looking very seriously at monitor screens. I held Kate's hand, asked her how she was and what had happened. She couldn't remember everything but told me the horse was spooked by some walkers and bucked, she fell off and it had trampled on her tummy and arm. Her arm was shredded. A real mess.

But the biggest concern was her abdominal pain.

A surgeon took me to one side. He said there was fluid in the abdominal cavity and he suspected it was blood from the aorta. He also thought the bowel was ripped but wouldn't know for sure until they opened her up.

That's when it hit home, it was major surgery to save her life! He said they needed to get her in quickly, that there would be three surgeons, two to operate on the blood leak and the bowel and one other to repair her arm. They needed Kate to sign a consent form. I was shaking and went over to her and told her what they were going to do.

Kate said, 'Oh bloody hell, do I have to? Is it that bad?' I offered to sign it, as she was really in no fit state, but they insisted she did. She couldn't read it, so they read it out, basically warning of the dangers of surgery anaesthesia and death! She did her best to sign it and that was it, they wheeled her away. I kissed her goodbye, I didn't even know if I'd see her again.

The vascular surgeon who had told me what they were going to do said he expected it would be a 4- to 5-hour operation, so I should go home and someone would ring me when it was over. What else could I do? Ann was waiting outside the pre-op room. She was just as shocked as I, and for once didn't swear! 'Come on,' she said 'let's get you home.'

The drive home with Ann was fortunately not as scary. It was now 5pm and I had animals to feed and check. I was under instructions that as soon as I heard anything, to ring her. I completed my farm work, had a shower and sat with my phone. I'd made sure it was charged and in a part of the house where we could get reception.

It was a lovely evening. I decided to sit outside on the patio with a cup of tea. We live in a very rural area and it is so quiet. I jumped as the phone rang. I looked at the screen: 'No caller ID'. This was it. I knew it would be the hospital. My heart started to beat so hard I could almost hear it banging on my chest.

I pressed the green button and spoke a brief 'Hello'. I could hardly speak and was fearing bad news. The caller announced himself as a surgeon at James Cook. He said they had completed the internal surgery. The aorta was ruptured but they had managed to stitch it. There was some bowel damage which they had also repaired. He also reported the orthopaedic surgeon was operating on her arm but that Kate was out of immediate danger and everything had gone very well. He said, 'We are just stitching her up now.'

Crikey! I had visions of him stood there with a phone tucked under his chin, head on one side, all his surgeon regalia on and a needle and thread in his hand stitching my wife up!

I sat down on the patio wall, thanked him profusely and asked his assurance about her condition. He said she was very lucky as the aorta hadn't been too badly damaged, but this had been a major op and she would be going into the high dependence unit (HDU) to recuperate. He said I could visit later, but naturally she would be very sleepy.

I rang Ann who said she would come round and take me. It was about 6pm but we didn't leave till 8pm to give her time to be taken to HDU.

I started to call everyone. Kate's parents and brother, my parents and family. At least I had good news even though she'd had major surgery.

We got to the hospital about 9pm. Ann parked correctly this time and we waited till 10pm before they would let us see her. The HDU is very specialised, with one nurse per patient. Kate had tubes everywhere and her arm bandaged. She was extremely tired and said she was sorry she couldn't make my tea! Typical Kate!

It is really upsetting to see someone you love in this

state, but also very comforting to know we have fantastic people within the NHS. The vascular surgeon who repaired the aorta had been called in specially to do this operation and it was Sunday afternoon, his day off.

Kate remained in hospital for 8 nights. I travelled daily to see her and was so pleased when she eventually came home. But there was a long journey ahead. She had a minimum of 6 months before she was back to normal.

While she'd been in hospital our cat had given birth to kittens in the barn and once Kate got home she loved walking down to see them every day. It was like a little challenge to try and get her strength back just by walking a few steps. The main thing was that she could cook though, so I got my tea!

We hadn't planned a holiday but booked ourselves to Menorca for a week at the end of September and, apart from the travelling, it proved to be a great boost to get a little bit of sunshine.

Kate made a full recovery although it was obviously slow going at times and yes, she was back out riding, not on Tilly though, she was sold and replaced with a much more sedate horse called Lorna who she loves.

Phew! It was a tough time for Kate, but what wonderful friends we have. Everyone offered to help if needed. That's special.

CHAPTER 31

Dad

My family mean the world to me. We're not a big family by any means but we're close. I can't ever remember any of us falling out. My childhood was very loving and and I hope that I brought that to my two boys and in turn, that they can carry it on with their families.

It's always sad when a family member dies. My grandad Bob Jeffery and my nana going I've already told you about. Aunt Ellen, who I had stayed with in Africa, died in her late seventies. Even though she was a nurse she chose to smoke heavily. It was a wonder she lived as long really. She lived in a bungalow in Haxby after selling the place in Ilfracombe to return to be nearer family. She had no family other than us.

My two sons, Robert and David, and I have become real good mates over the years as we have grown up together. They helped me through a very bad time. We have had some very special times together. I'm not so sure I could ever forgive them for the introduction to Heaven in Magaluf though! They are a credit to themselves and I am immensely proud of them both. Their wives Romany and Ann-Marie are very good at helping my mum now she is on her own. They are the loveliest daughters-in- law I could wish for.

My brother Andy lives in Germany with his wife Monica. They have three sons, Christian, Mikey and Kevin. My brother David lives in Luxembourg with his wife Jane. David left the RAF and works for NATO. I always kid him about his job as he cannot tell us what he actually does!

He has done exceedingly well. Their two sons Peter and Harry live in Sheffield. My youngest brother Ian lives in York with his wife Ann. Ian is still running a milk delivery business and has recently started a Christmas tree growing business. He hopes to have his first crop ready by Christmas 2021.

My two sons have three sons between them: Robert and his wife Romany have Marley; David and his wife Ann-Marie have Ryan and William. We are very much a male family, so when Romany delivered a baby girl in 2014 we were all elated, and I was especially for my mum who had tried all those years ago for a girl. Little Maisie Jeffery is the apple of everyone's eye! And, while writing this book Robert and Romany have also added to their family with another lovely baby boy called Maddox!

My uncle John and aunt Wendy had two children, Nicholas and Jayne. They're married with family too. Wendy needs care now as she has Parkinson's, but she still takes great care of herself and is always smiling. Uncle John is 80 this year (2020) and has recently moved to Yarm to be nearer his daughter after living in Wigginton since 1947.

Mum and Dad lived in their detached bungalow in Old Earswick for 25 years after selling Scriven House Farm. It was perfect for them with a lovely big garden and close to shops and doctors. When my boys were young Dad really took to Robert. I suppose his first grandchild was really special. He loved them both of course.

Dad was so much better at being a dad and grandad than me. He loved us all equally, but never showed it or told us, but we knew he did.

When he got to 84 he decided he and Mum should downsize, sell the bungalow in Old Earswick and move into a smaller bungalow in Haxby where everything, including family, were within walking distance. It was

December when they moved and I was so upset for them. I knew Dad was preparing things for when he wasn't here and that it would be better for Mum to be in a small manageable bungalow in a big village than the bungalow in Old Earswick.

It was September 2016 when Dad first started complaining about lower abdominal pain. Mum had spent years nursing and she was worried. They managed to get him in for a scan fairly quickly. It was pancreatic cancer.

Dad was offered a biopsy to see if there was a chance it could be treated but he declined. He knew, as we all did, that this was going to take him. The next few weeks were very hard and very challenging. Dad started to deteriorate quite rapidly and lost a lot of weight. He wasn't very big anyway and soon he was struggling to even stand. Mum was doing her best to feed him but of course he had no appetite.

Andy and Monica came over from Germany. This was heart-wrenching because when they left, Dad knew he wouldn't ever see Andy again. It's the only time I have ever seen Dad cry.

We were all there to see Andy and Monica off, but we knew that we would be seeing them again soon. It got to the point where Dad needed 24-hour care and we thought about a hospice, but Mum wouldn't hear of it. Marie Curie nurses got involved and between us and them, but especially Mum, we looked after him at home. I remember sitting with him in those final days and he said to me, 'I must get that bloody radiator fixed for your mother before I snuff it!'

That's how he was, no 'I love you' and 'I'm so upset' or anything like that, just fix that bloody radiator!

It was Thursday December 15, 2016 and Mum had someone staying over to help her get some sleep. I travelled down from the farm as I had daily for the past few weeks. It was an awful journey knowing every time when I got there Dad would be worse. He was never going to get better.

If any of my animals had been like he was at the end I would have had them put to sleep humanely. I arrived at 8.30am and the nurse was there making a cup of tea for Mum who was in the front room. Dad had been bedbound for over a week and was now in a special bed delivered only a couple of days ago by the council. It could be moved up and down and had sides on it to keep him more comfortable.

I looked in on him. He looked terrible. I sat with Mum. The nurse went back to Dad for a while. After a few minutes she came in and told us we should sit with him as his breathing had changed.

My heart pounded as I knew what was going to happen. We went into his room and sat, one at each side of the bed. He was hardly breathing and I took his hand and held it. His fingers had gone white and I thought to myself how much work those hands must have done over the years. I held his hand while he drew his last breath with Mum bent over him sobbing her heart out.

I was so glad I was there with Mum at the end. Mum, Dad and me. His first born.

He was 86, had enjoyed his life without too much ill health and had been the best dad anyone could have wished for. I wish I could be half as good as him.

His funeral took place on my birthday, 4 January 2017, and my cousin Julie, who is a vicar, took the service at York Crematorium. My 3 brothers and I carried the coffin. My 2 sons Robert and David escorted Mum. I read his favourite Psalm 'The Lord is my Shepherd'. He had always told me he wanted that at his funeral. The place was packed. His final song that he loved, that Kate and I had at our wedding, was played at the end, 'I Love You

Because' by Jim Reeves.

A few days later Mum and I collected the ashes and my brother Ian, me and Mum scattered them in a favourite place where Mum and Dad used to visit years ago. I loved him dearly and think about him every day.

William George Jeffery, Bill, my dad, my hero.

For me, there is nothing as important as family. We all face challenges in life and to have the friendship and love of family around you is a very wonderful thing. I have been and remain very lucky in that respect.

Chris the family man!

CHAPTER 32

Back to Business

Kate and I spent much of our time and money buying Spring View Farm and then over the next 2-3 years working every hour available and investing even more time in completely renovating the property, the garden and creating our small farm with rare breed livestock.

We had been so focused on the farm that we took our eye off the ball at Green's. I'd go to work, but then I'd be back home for 10 o'clock, leaving everyone else to it. I'd be back, riving out fences and tending our animals. I loved it. I had the bit firmly between my teeth in getting on at home, but the only problem there was that it wasn't making us any money. You can spend ages building up a business, but then when you take your foot off the pedal it can turn the other way.

One thing I have to say is the team we've had at Green's has always been fantastic, right from when there were just three of us. They're our friends as well as being part of the business. It's just that our focus, and particularly mine, had gone on to the farm and building our new life. That was the new, fun and exciting bit.

Green's was still doing well and in terms of business turnover it was continually expanding, but so were our overheads and the business was not making enough profit. Something needed to be done.

In May 2018 we were approached by BATA, a long-established farmers' co-operative supplying similar products as ourselves and with several shops and stores across Yorkshire. They were a lot larger than us and wanted to buy the business.

Kate and I thought this would provide the answer to our problems in one go. We accepted their offer and agreed to sell. It was going to clear our mortgage and we would have money left to develop the farm.

We had to sign the usual non-disclosure agreements and start a due diligence process, which proved a nightmare. I understood BATA needed to be diligent, but their consultants took so much time that it ended up causing us real problems at work as, during that time, we weren't able to tell our team. Rumours started and the atmosphere became really bad.

Some were asking if we were going bust, closing down or selling up and we couldn't say anything. It was a dreadful time.

Then came the sucker punch. At a meeting with BATA in their accountants' office in October 2018 they withdrew their offer. I felt they had taken us for a ride. Their CEO was apologetic, but we were simply disgusted.

Surely they must have known if they could afford to buy us or not before making a written formal offer for the business?

Kate and I left that meeting not quite knowing what to do next. We had been planning our exit from the business in good faith and with a firm offer on the table, subject to this due diligence. We now had an unsettled team, a customer base that was very unsure about us and we owed a substantial figure for work that had proven to be unnecessary.

Since we were now back to square one, considering our future but without what seemed a lifeline from BATA, Kate and I made a decision to downsize the business. We looked at all the figures, decided that big wasn't beautiful and made some hard decisions.

One of our key team members had become unsettled

and handed his notice in. He'd said he was returning to work on his father's farm, but he has set up in business doing the same as us just down the road. It happens. That's business. After all, we left Laycock's when the opportunity arose with Ray Green's.

Three of the team were made redundant. It wasn't nice doing that but they all got jobs elsewhere quite quickly so that was good. We sold three vehicles and stopped any farm deliveries which were costly. We reduced our stock from £400,000 to £200,000 and reduced our rent significantly by giving notice on part of the area we rented. We knew we would lose sales by doing all of this, but our overheads were going to be reduced also and our business plan showed we would actually make more profit.

We closed all branches other than Thirsk and relocated all stock and offices into one building, the original building we had taken when we moved there in 2006. Hopefully this would set us up for a more profitable business as we planned to work smarter not harder. In retrospect we had too many outlets and although sales were going well, we had found ourselves chasing sales rather than chasing profit.

By the end of 2019 the business was much more streamlined, efficient and amazingly, just as profitable. It had become easier to manage and not as stressful. The whole business has been transformed and we are now concentrating on profit not turnover!

I still long to be on the farm every day and try to work it that way, but 2018 specifically was the year when we refocused on Green's.

One of the reasons we have done so well over the years is down to our team. You cannot run something successfully without good people around you and we were very fortunate to have people like Mike Foster who was a great supporter of myself and Kate. Mike worked for us for a lot of years and ran our Northallerton branch in its heyday. He was highly thought of by all and like a father figure to others. He now has his own farm at Bishop Thornton near Ripon.

Hayley Wood has been with us many years and her versatility is amazing. From driving a forklift to serving in the shop, producing lazer tags and answering customers' queries she does it all, and with a smile on her face. Hayley is married to Richard and they have a daughter Jovi who has spent a lot of time with us at Green's during lockdown as chief dog walker! Richard comes at Christmas to help us with the Christmas trees.

Dave Gill came to us from Farmway. People were coming in to the shop in Thirsk saying I had to have Dave on board. I met him, I agreed, he joined us and he brought so much business. Dave, also known as Golly, had a major heart operation in the winter of 2019/20 but he's back with us now. The number of good wishes he received on Facebook and in the store was proof, if it was needed, of his popularity. He's literally the king of customer service! He's been in the industry all his life and is married to Lyn. They live in Sowerby, next to Thirsk.

Carol Cornforth is our country store manager. Carol is ultra-reliable and extremely knowledgeable. She's married to a farmer, Pete, and loves riding out with her daughter Elizabeth.

Our other team members include Kayleigh Rudd, who is Carol's assistant; Jane Towse; Melanie, who is Kate's cousin and helps with admin; and 'Saturday boy' Louis.

They are all so important to our success and are all 'key workers' for us throughout the pandemic.

Anna Butler has recently left the business. She was a really professional person and helped Kate and I tremendously. We both wish her well for the future.

CHAPTER 33

Farmer Chris – On the Farm

Today our livestock farm is currently focused on our beautiful pedigree Whitebred Shorthorn herd and the Plum Pudding pigs, our Oxford Sandy & Blacks. I'm still involved with pigs after all these years, having started with them at Askham Bryan College all those years ago and having first made my career with them in North and East Yorkshire, Suffolk and Northern Ireland.

My love affair with the rare Whitebred Shorthorn breed started when we saw them at the Great Yorkshire Show in 2015. Although the breed's origin is a bit sketchy it started out being called either the Cumberland White or Cumberland Shorthorn in the 19th century and is a completely separate breed to either the Beef Shorthorn or Dairy Shorthorn, ideal for conservation grazing on hill pastures.

Whitebred Shorthorns are bred mainly in the border counties of England and Scotland, specifically across north-west England and south-west Scotland. They have an outer coat of creamy/white soft hair and a thick mossy undercoat.

The Whitebred Shorthorn bull is bred primarily as a crossing bull to mate with any breed of female, but principally with the Galloway to produce the Blue Grey, and the Highland producing a Cross Highlander, its progeny being hardy and hill worthy.

I said if we got to a herd of 10 Whitebred Shorthorn cows I would be happy, but we are now just over that figure so I may have to re-think. Having more cows means having more calves each year, which means a multiplication of the herd over the years, particularly if you have calves that look so good you just have to keep some of them. And that all leads to needing more land for them to graze.

Of course, then there are the moments that come up that you least expect – and I'm not talking about coronavirus here, which became an issue just as I was nearing completion of this book. No, what I'm talking about was something much more invigorating and exciting.

This is where our neighbour Richard Greenwood deserves a special mention. Richard rented the farm buildings here before we bought the farm and has become a very good friend, an ally and a big help. When we've been away he has looked after our livestock and if I need anything he's always there.

In October 2018, around the same time as we were going through hell with the collapse of the deal with BATA, Richard told me, 'There's one of your cows to sell in York Market.' He'd seen a photograph. I'd told him it wouldn't be a Whitebred Shorthorn, more likely it would be a White Park. He came back and said it was definitely a Whitebred Shorthorn.

They are that rare you don't see them just in a normal weekly sale. The sale was the following day, so I rang the Whitebred Shorthorn Association, the breed society, and asked whether they were aware of a Whitebred Shorthorn going into a sale at York. They said they'd only just got wind of it.

I went along the next day, absolutely as excited as I could be, because you never see a Whitebred Shorthorn just coming up at a regular weekly sale and that would mean the regulars at the market would probably not be interested. When I got to the mart, as early as I could, I took a look before the sale and there were 2 or 3 Whitebred

Shorthorns, but more specifically this one registered cow and one registered bull. That meant they were both pure pedigrees. This was a really lucky break.

The bull wasn't in great shape. I thought he looked like he could be good and so for assurance I rang the breed society and asked what was going on with the bull. They gave me the original breeder's name and it was well-known breeder Donald Hendry from Dumfries. I rang Donald and told him there was a bull for sale called Ben Ledi Duke. He told me to buy the bull. He told me his genetics went back 30-40 years and I could not get the bloodline anywhere else.

By now my excitement had gone through the roof! I was going to bid for an animal that probably wouldn't have any other of my breed society members there, which could mean getting Duke at a great price.

I don't hear particularly well, so I practised. I went into the ring, sat in the appropriate place and sat up so that I could hear what the auctioneer Edward Stephenson was saying.

The cow came in first and only got to just short of £300. I bought it. That was a steal. Then the bull came in, Duke. I bought him for £700. What a day! And all thanks to Richard for tipping me off. I even bought another cow with a calf at foot, so I had four to get home. I didn't have a trailer with me so on the way home I borrowed a trailer from Rob Dent.

I kid you not if you see Ben Ledi Duke today he is the best example of a pedigree Whitebred Shorthorn bull I have ever seen, bred by one of the best breeders in the UK. I can quite understand why Donald just said, 'Buy him.' He is stunning. I've used him on all my cows, except one as she's his daughter. If I had the time to show him I would – and he would win. We're looking at registering him with Genus to collect semen and sell straws, he's that good. He's great not just for Whitebred cows but for heifers on dairy farms as it is a very easy calving breed.

And to give you an idea of who holds the purse strings still today Kate had told me, remember what we were going through at the time at Green's, that I'd have to borrow the money from my mum who lives in the very built-up area of Wigginton.

I pulled in with my pickup and trailer after I'd collected the trailer from Rob and said, 'Mum, Kate won't let me have them unless you loan me the money,' and she wrote me a cheque. To be fair Kate couldn't believe what I'd got for my money. It was an amazing stroke of luck.

You can't just carry on multiplying your numbers of cattle year on year. We sell stock to other breeders. We've sold bulls entire to others, to breed from, and we sold three very nice heifers earlier this year (2020) at Carlisle.

Our acreage at Spring View Farm is 10 acres and we also have 8 acres at Wigginton. Late in 2019 I negotiated a deal for a further 9 acres at Oulston nearby, so we're heading upwards on the grassland we have available for our stock and thanks to our neighbours and good friends Tim and Ann Robson it looks like we will have a greater acreage very soon.

We presently have 3 Oxford Sandy & Black sows which we AI. We try to farrow them together which makes for a busy period when pigs are all born around the same time. The last sow to farrow had 17 piglets. Kate's spent the best part of 2-3 nights with them. Many of them fed from a bottle. I pulled out 15 of them. She had two herself.

Our other rare breeds are Kerry Hill, Hebridean and Border Leicester sheep and Belted Galloway cattle.

Over the period of a few years when we put in a monumental effort at Spring View to the detriment of Green's we massively improved the property and the farm and that has put on value at Thornton on the Hill.

Farming, Celebs and Plum Pudding Pigs!

Our hope is that one day we can retire or semi-retire from Green's and have enough going on at Spring View Farm, through such as a farm shop selling our own rare breed meats, tea room, shepherd's huts, holiday lets, pony trekking and open farm days.

Kate and I have made some preliminary targets for when we'd like to have achieved this and we're aiming to start open farm days when coronavirus is out of the way.

CHAPTER 34

Celebs on the Farm – Series 1

In March 2018 I received a call from Lou Cowmeadow of Daisybeck Studios in Leeds, the TV company that makes *The Yorkshire Vet*. Lou said, 'Chris, a friend of mine Richard Woolfe is making a show called *Celebs on the Farm* and has asked if I know anybody in Yorkshire who would be the judge. I've told him you'll do it.'

I said, 'What are you talking about? What do you mean, you've told him I'd do it?' I was excited, but to go on television? Lou just reassured me, 'Yes, Chris, you'll be fantastic, trust me.'

At that precise moment I said I would think about it. Sixty seconds later I thought to myself, 'Are you mad!? You've been given an opportunity at 60 years old to go and make a TV show. Why wouldn't you do it? I remember talking to myself like this, saying, 'You love working with Julian. You love being in front of the camera on *The Yorkshire Vet*, why would you not love this?' My heart was pounding. I rang Lou and told her I was in.

Richard rang half an hour later. He's a really colourful, very well-known, well-respected guy who has been in the TV world for over 30 years. He produced *That's Life* with Esther Rantzen and ran Sky 1 for many years. Richard told me about the show and that he wanted a farmer to judge a group of celebrities doing lots of different tasks on a farm. I said I wasn't an actor, but he just said he wanted me to be myself and would I come down to London to meet the rest of the production team, or they could come up to York.

The way it worked out was a FaceTime discussion with Richard and his producer Simon Procter in London and me in my car outside Green's. It was pretty much an interview. I asked if they'd seen the comedy moment with Elsie and Julian. They hadn't, but they liked me. They rang back later after they'd spoken with Channel 5. By then they'd looked at everything I'd done on *The Yorkshire Vet* and welcomed me on board.

Farmer Chris was born!

Everything moved quickly. I was booked on a train to King's Cross the following week where I was picked up by Goowoo Media, the production company owned by Richard Woolfe and Paul Goodliffe. I was taken to Camden where I met them in the upstairs room of a pub, along with Simon Procter and two or three admin assistants. It was all going well. Wine, beer, lunch – and then in walked the young man who was to become my new best friend.

We were all talking away when Stephen made his entrance. Stephen Bailey. Stand-up comedian and TV presenter. He was holding a bunch of flowers and in typical Stephen-style, very effeminate, said, 'Hi Guuuyys! Stephen here!' Very flamboyant.

I'm thinking, OMG this guy is so camp. I'd never heard of him and had no idea the show's presenter was going to be a camp comedian. We hit it off immediately. We are chalk and cheese but bounced off each other straight away and I knew I was going to enjoy working with him. He had an aura about him.

Stephen was dressed quite smartly and when he spoke it was like listening to a 55-year-old woman who had smoked all her life! Now that I know him after two series of *Celebs*, to me he's a cross between Larry Grayson and Graham Norton with a bit of Julian Clary chucked in. He is such a warm, friendly, funny young man and is going places! He made me feel extremely welcome and we got talking about the show straight away.

I think what the production team wanted to see was how we would get on. They wanted the presenter and judge to have a good rapport. I felt there was an instant chemistry. They FaceTimed one of the Channel 5 executives and went through the format of the show. I found out who the celebs were going to be, not that I knew any of them! I found out the show would be filmed on a farm in East Sussex and when to be there – filming was due to start the first week of May for two weeks.

I was still in shock that I was there, in London, talking with a TV production company that was making a show I was going to feature in with the young man who was to become my new best friend, the very intellectual and articulate Stephen Bailey, the most camp person I have ever known (although Louie Spence comes a close second). Stephen lives in Tooting but comes from Manchester originally. I felt he was going to be a big hit on the show with his effervescent and original banter and that we would get on well together.

Stephen is in his early 30s and has become like a son to me. He has often joked about me being his screen dad (amongst other things!).

In a short space of time I was transported from a world of perhaps selling our business to BATA and working with my cattle and pigs to a completely different world of making a TV series.

We were due to start filming on the Monday afternoon and Kate travelled down with me for a couple of nights. It was a lovely, hot weekend and we stayed over on the way down on the Saturday night. We had Peggy, my Jack Russell terrier who goes with me wherever I go. The next night we stayed at the hotel in Rye where I have stayed for the duration of the two series so far.

Kate came with me to have a look at the farm and

we met the farmer Andrew (Dunlop), his wife Linda and Jamie who works with them. I got a feel for the farm, workmen were everywhere putting up *Celebs on the Farm* banners and suddenly everything was real. What had I done? I thought, tomorrow I've to go in front of camera.

I took Kate to Ashford railway station on Monday morning where she took the train to London Victoria and then hopped over to King's Cross to get back home and leaving me to it with Peggy. Unfortunately, her train broke down on the way. Not a happy lady.

The celebs began arriving from lunchtime onwards. This beautiful East Sussex barn had been converted into a studio setting where all the morning briefings and evening eliminations would take place.

Lunsford Farm is a 300-acre sheep and cattle farm near to the south coast in the village of Pett, just west of Rye and east of Hastings. It's set around what are known as the Pett Levels, which are hundreds of acres of flat grassland, reclaimed land from the sea with drainage ditches everywhere. It's a big livestock farming area with really fertile land. The Dunlops also run a glamping site and Lunsford has been used several times for TV location filming. It is stunningly beautiful.

The celebs all had checked shirts and boots provided. I had asked what I was to wear for filming, but all I was told was just to come as a farmer. Being me, I wanted to create an image so mine was going to be jeans, work boots, checked shirt, gilet, flat cap and crook. They loved the shepherd's crook, which was the afterthought. I'd been a bit unsure of what to do with my hands and the crook was the perfect answer.

As I was the 'henchman', the guy that was to boot the celebs off the farm one by one, a bit like Lord Sugar does on *The Apprentice*, the producer only wanted me to be seen properly by the celebs for the first time when they were close to being on camera. I was hidden in the production office (a Portakabin at the back of the cowshed) while Stephen was their first point of contact and did all the meeting and greeting.

Once all the celebs were on site, had been met by Stephen and were getting used to their accommodation in motorhomes, Stephen and I were brought together. We were given a small script, we practised, and then it was time. Camera, lights, action!

By now my rectal artery and anal passage were having a field day – eat your heart out Stephen! There were people everywhere – cameramen, lighting crew, sound. I had all my Farmer Chris gear on and was ready to go. Stephen was having his eye shadow put on, a bit of rouge, applying his lippy, manicure, all that sort of thing! I was taken into the barn and was loitering in the shadows behind the bales. The celebs were now on the bales preparing for lift off!

Although I thought I wouldn't know any of them, I knew Lorraine Chase and Gleb Savchenko because Kate and I do watch *Strictly*, but I had no idea who the rest of them were. Lorraine saw me in the shadows and must have read what I was thinking and seen my fear because she came over to me and said in that wonderfully charming way she has: 'Hello my darling. Are you alright? Don't worry, you'll be fine. We're only normal people you know.' With that she went back to where the rest of the celebs were sat. What a nice thing of her to do.

Stephen went into the barn. The cameras were rolling. Do they still roll? Anyway, he began his introduction to the show and then came the point where he mentioned a 'very important person' he was about to introduce to the celebs. This was the point where I came in, on screen for the first time as Farmer Chris.

My first thought was to mind the bloody step I had to walk over to get into the main part of the barn/studio. I was determined my entrance (don't smile Stephen, it's only a word) was not going to be compromised. All the celebs applauded and I tried to remember the script. Stephen was very good and basically held my hand through it all (I can see you giving me that look again now Stephen).

'I'm Farmer Chris from Yorkshire,' I said. 'I'm very sorry, but I've no idea who the hell you lot are.' They smiled. I got them all to tell me who they were and we gave them their first challenge designed to help them find their way around the farm and get used to their surroundings. Once I'd finished that first set up, I felt a lot better. Farmer Chris was under way!

On set Stephen is a huge help. Before we record a scene, whether it is to start the day or it is elimination time, we go off and find a quiet part of the farm to go over our lines. This is often very nerve-racking for me as I'm the one who makes the decision on who is eliminated and who receives the 'best in show' rosettes that I present each day. I don't have any autocues or script boards and sometimes in the heat of the moment Stephen will step in with a prompt, for which I am always grateful.

We have received so many compliments from the viewers about our on-screen rapport that I can now see why they chose a gruff Yorkshire farmer and a camp Manchester comedian to front the show. It really works.

I'd been asked by the production team to be quite hard on the celebs, very strict, and for the first two or three days of filming they also had me eating with the crew rather than the celebs. After the first three or four days I was with the celebs more off camera, as they then wanted me to warm to them.

It's only when you are part of a TV programme you realise just how much else is involved other than the filming. While I didn't sit directly with the celebs at first when it was mealtimes everyone eats together in a big, open cart shed with all catering brought in. Nevertheless, it still amazed me at the time how many were there. As well as the production crew, the celebs and me, there were two big security guards looking after the celebs, at least two medics on site all the time and many more that I didn't know what the hell their jobs were.

Richard (Woolfe) told me that, years ago, before today's technology, there would have been double the amount of people for a show like this.

On the third day of filming, the barn used for the morning briefing and evening elimination scenes was transformed into a photo studio. Channel 5Star brought in their PR teams and set the place up for promotional shots of the celebs, Stephen and I. This took all afternoon and most of the evening and it took hours for Megan and Charlotte to get ready. They brought in their own hair stylists and makeup teams! When I saw the girls, the result was truly unbelievable. I had never seen anyone look so perfect. They almost looked as though they weren't human.

That's when it struck me that this TV world malarkey really is a whole different world and I love it!

There were 8 celebs in the first series and first to receive their 'notice to quit' from Farmer Chris was Sandi Bogle of Channel 4's *Gogglebox* show. I really did enjoy working with everyone, but Sandi, although a lovely person, just didn't seem to have the energy after three days.

Lovely Megan McKenna was next to go. Megan was the easiest to get rid of because she simply couldn't do the task. She was going out with the sadly now no longer with us Mike 'Muggy' Thalassitis from ITV2's *Love Island* at the time and he came to pick her up for a night out during our time on the farm.

This was one of the things I didn't like about Series 1. I'd thought the idea was for the celebs to remain on the farm, apart from the middle weekend when everyone could go home, but several went out for meals during the week. This didn't happen in Series 2. Megan has gone on to wonderful things, winning *X Factor Celebrity* and she's touring with Lionel Richie this year.

Next to face the Farmer Chris axe was Lorraine, who I liked very much, because of what she had done for me that first day but also because she is really such a nice person.

It was my next two eliminations that caused quite a bit of a going on really. I had to leave us with three from five on the penultimate day, which meant getting rid of two. This was set to be my biggest moment on the show.

I knew who the final 3 were going to be, but it didn't include Charlotte Dawson, the only girl now left in the show. I'd booted off all the girls! (Stephen, stop that, I can see you grinning from here!)

I'd been told all along that the decision was mine on all eliminations and awarding of 'best in show' rosettes. There is always a meeting in the production office with myself, Stephen and the producers before each elimination so that we know what we are all doing, but the decision was still mine – or so I thought!

Richard came to me that day and said 'the channel' wanted a female in the final as it would be good for viewing figures and credibility. I said, 'What about my credibility! I'm a judge, you've asked me to judge what I've seen and as much as I love her I can't put Charlotte into the final,' and in my opinion there had been no girl good enough to be in it. Charlotte was fantastic to work with, daft as a brush at times and very nice, but she couldn't do what I'd wanted her to do, so she had to go.

Richard looked most displeased with this and stormed off announcing he would have to speak with 'the channel'. There were hissy fits going on and I was just about in tears of frustration, because I was making an honest decision.

This is the closest we've ever come to falling out. We are great friends and even ended up on holiday together in a roundabout way. What I like most about GooWoo is the way the two directors get involved in everything, like I do back home. Richard and Paul are very 'hands-on' even to the point of getting the motorhomes and the canteen ready before the celebs arrive. They had both made me feel very much at home up until then.

I was upset that my credibility was at stake here and I knew clearly that Ashley, Bobby and Gleb had to be in the final. Charlotte, who I adored, simply wasn't good enough to be in it. I wasn't going to walk off the set. I'd stood my ground but was quite unsure what was going to happen next. Were the programme's producers and 'the channel' going to force me to back down? I seriously considered walking off if they did!

Richard came back after a few minutes and he could see I was quite upset. He sat down with me and said he'd spoken to 'the channel' and that I'd got their backing. The channel and GooWoo. 'You're absolutely right, it's your decision. You're the judge and the jury.'

Paul was there too, a lovely man and very quiet. He hugged me and told me I was a good man and that he fully supported me. Phew! That was quite an emotional moment. I had felt an enormous amount of pressure on me as a judge, but it had been nothing compared to that moment.

My own humble feeling is that if GooWoo and 'the channel' had wanted a female in the final they should have had a female that was capable of getting to the final. They had gone for people who had a big following on social media, which I can understand and have since embraced it myself, people like Megan and Charlotte, but they hadn't thought it through completely. It was, what we all know when we are doing something new, a bit of a

Farming, Celebs and Plum Pudding Pigs!

learning curve for all of us.

After all that rumpus it was time to say goodbye to Charlotte and Louie Spence. For all Louie's undoubted TV appeal and personality extraordinaire he was not going to be my farming champion. I hadn't known him at all at the start but when my sons heard about him being on the show, after we'd finished filming, they told me, 'Dad, he's crazy,' which he was. He's an amazingly flamboyant character, especially for a brusque Yorkshire farmer!

Nonetheless I always find the eliminations very emotional because we have all got to know each other over the period we are together and it was still sad to see Charlotte and Louie going, but I had my final 3. Louie did okay anyway because he appeared in the spin-off *Celebs on the Ranch* set in the States, which Stephen also presented – and he won it! Well done Louie!

That left us with Ashley McKenzie, a Commonwealth gold medallist, World Cup champion and Team GB Olympian; Bobby Cole Norris from the ITV2 show known as *TOWIE* (*The Only Way Is Essex*); and Gleb Savchenko from BBC1's *Strictly Come Dancing*.

Ashley was up every morning, out on the farm, helping Farmer Andrew feed the sheep, putting in extra shifts. He just loved it and is a lovely, passionate guy. Bobby had come on so well. He'd had a problem with his ankle being bitten by horseflies and it had been badly swollen. It was terrible, but he'd battled through it. He could hardly walk but was no wimp. He'd stood out for me, never stopping asking questions about farming and about my farm. He was interested, talking with me as much behind the scenes as well as in front of camera. Gleb was Mr Cool. Everything I gave him he did very well and was without doubt the best of the 3 as a farmer.

I could have given the Series 1 title to any of the three. I was sat deliberating over who I was going to give the title and told Richard I was struggling making my decision. Did I give it to someone who had made the biggest improvement from the start? The most willing?

Richard said, 'I'll tell you what to do. If you were going away tomorrow, which of these three would you want to stay at home and look after your farm?' I had my answer immediately. It had to be Gleb. Richard said, 'There's your winner then.'

I spent a fabulous two weeks on location at Andrew's farm and staying over in the hotel in Rye with Peggy. It felt quite surreal working with people who made television shows for a living, being on set appearing in one. I'd been transported from my world of farming in Yorkshire to an entirely different world where many were gay, spoke in words like, 'Are you alright, babe?' and, 'Yes darling,' with lots of kissing and cuddling and, 'I love yous,' with an incredible feeling of warmth, of family.

We live in the same country, but this was a different world and I loved it, I absolutely loved it. At one point I may have even embraced it all a little too much for some of them. I'd started calling them 'babe' and 'darling' too! Someone said, 'Farmer Chris, please ...' I was in their bubble, having a fun time. I really enjoyed talking with and working with people like Bobby, Louie and Lorraine. Bobby was really upset in the end when he didn't win, which was a shame, but there can only be one winner.

And I was treated really well throughout. The runners are there to get anything anyone wants or needs from a bottle of water to suncream, chocolate or more clothing. On my first day my sunglasses fell apart. The tiny screw that holds them together had fallen out and I didn't have it. One of the runners asked if I would like my 'shades' mending and by the end of the day I had them back and fixed!

I discovered that being a runner is one way to get a job

with a TV production company. It's the first step on a very long ladder and is where Stephen had started!

It had been just before we started filming the show that I had discovered I was to be called Farmer Chris. I wasn't sure about this at first as I didn't think Chris was a great farming name. I'd wondered about whether I should take on my old name with the Fab 4 and call myself Farmer Sid or Farmer Bill after my dad. These names sounded better somehow, but then I thought, why alter my name for goodness' sake!

It wasn't long before I was shortened to FC by the production team and the celebs off camera. It had been Bobby who had started it and it had stuck. Everyone on the show now calls me FC. (In some circles that may not be a good thing, but we'll leave that there.)

When we'd finished filming the show it was straight back to North Yorkshire for me until August when I went down to London for the press launch before the show was to air for the first time on Channel 5Star on August 20, 2018. Amidst all the hoo-hah we had going on back home over the possible sale of Green's, this was something good.

I was put up in a hotel in Camden and met up with Stephen, Richard, Paul and series producer Simon Procter at a pub in Camden Town before we took a taxi to the press launch party in London's West End. I'd been asked to wear my Farmer Chris look as the press would want photographs of me as I appear in the show. It felt a bit odd, dressed as a farmer in London's West End, but I was back in my TV bubble where everything is a bit different to 'up north'. I had my flat cap, but not my crook. That seemed a bit over the top.

Everyone was back together for the launch at this swish hotel. I was just as excited and nervous as I'd been back in May when I'd first arrived on the set at Lunsford Farm, as I didn't know quite what to expect. The launch party started at 7 o'clock and the press were all there. It was a big cocktail party with all the major newspapers and broadcast media and today's new media experts, the bloggers. The chief executive of Channel 5Star was there too. It was a big night for me.

Me, being me, I was thinking about how many millions would be watching, but I was thinking back to those days when *Dad's Army* was on television and there were only three channels when every show seemed to achieve millions regardless. I was told quite clearly that a show like ours on Channel 5Star, if it achieved 250,000 viewers that was quite good today. At first, I thought that's no good to me, I want 13 million! But these guys know what they are doing and they know their market. They know to expect a certain number of viewers, which will bring in so much revenue.

The series ended up achieving better viewing figures than anyone had anticipated and it was Channel 5Star's best viewed show of the summer, so it performed well, not that we were all necessarily bothered too much that night as no-one would know at that time. The drinks flowed and everyone had a great night.

I'll never forget walking down a street in London with a very scantily clad Charlotte Dawson on one arm and Megan McKenna on the other, followed by someone known as Lady Nadia of Essex and reality TV fame with Stephen just behind as we left the hotel after the official press launch. Charlotte had this amazing dress that was like strips of leather. There was I with my flat cap and working boots!

The paparazzi were all there as we'd walked out of the hotel and were about to be whisked away to where GooWoo had booked a room above a pub in Camden where we all watched the first show in the series that would run for two weeks. The 'paps' were in front of us as we walked and were constantly directing the girls to walk in a certain way, flick their hair, smile or pout, so they could get 'that' picture for the next morning's newspapers. And there was I in between these beautiful girls! I thought, I'm having some of this, and as I started getting involved they shouted of me too! Farmer Chris! Honestly, it was like you see on the telly when celebs leave nightclubs in London.

Natalie Woods was there too. I've not mentioned Natalie up until this point. Natalie runs her own talent agency and books talent for TV shows and then looks after them while filming takes place, in case anyone needs something urgently. She is such a lovely person and I had got on with her really well.

Anyway, Natalie shouts to Megan as she was getting into the car, 'Megan! Make sure you pull your skirt down love, because you know what they'll be looking for!' That's what Natalie does, she's there for her people.

Massive screens were all around us and watching the show with everyone was the most amazing feeling. I really felt part of this TV family that people like Richard and Paul create with their TV shows and where very talented young men like Stephen become stars. Stephen really is going places. I've been to see his stand-up show and he's extremely funny. Richard and Paul have done it all in television and I shall be forever grateful to them for the opportunity they gave me through Lou at Daisybeck Studios.

It was the most incredible night and it was also when I noticed something that I've since taken on board. The GooWoo team and the celebs were saying things like 'we're trending'. This was fairly new to me. I'd maybe heard the phrase before but not really grasped the power of what 'trending' meant. I suddenly realised more about social media and today's publicity. It's not all about whether the paparazzi managed to get a flash of Megan's knickers, it's not about getting half a million viewers to the show, it's about what's happening on Twitter, Facebook, Instagram and a plethora of others.

I'd been critical, like many of us are, of people I'd never heard of earning their livelihoods from reality shows and had seen our celebs on their mobile phones texting and emailing seconds before the camera action started, but now I knew how it all worked. At the end of the show even I sat there with my phone taking a picture of my credit as 'Resident Farmer Chris Jeffery'.

And that was that. A fantastic night. The show was launched. I came home the following day and was back to reality – not a reality show, not that kind of reality. I was back to real reality. The show ran its course, achieved good figures, but that was it. It was a strange feeling being down there in London with all the hubbub of a TV show one minute and back in North Yorkshire selling animal food and mucking out pigs the next day!

CHAPTER 35

Celebs on the Farm – Series 2

How sad am I? When I found out there was to be the spin-off set in America called *Celebs on the Ranch* I wanted to be the rancher! I had to have a talk with myself again. I told myself I wasn't a rancher, I couldn't ride a horse and that I was being stupid. I was still gutted though. Stephen was going as presenter. Richard was going. Bobby and Louie went too – and Louie won! I was gutted not to get the gig even so.

I kept in touch with Stephen and we were both hoping to get a second series. I'd been up to see Stephen's show in Newcastle and he told me later that he knew it was on, but that he was under strict instructions to say nothing to anybody. What he had said though was that, 'If we get Series 2 it will be me and you, because it's our show.' The worst thing for me would have been if I had been dropped after Series 1.

It was February 2019 when I received a WhatsApp message from Richard: 'Hi Chris, great news. Series 2. I want you and Peggy down here again to film.'

I was ecstatic. I love being in that world. Series 1 had seen me going into the unknown and had been a massive challenge, taking me out of my comfort zone. Series 2 was to be a whole new ball game. I was the one who had done it all before. The celebs hadn't. I knew that going into the barn that first day I was to be the one to be feared, not the other way around. Lorraine would have been proud of me.

GooWoo booked myself and Peggy back into our hotel in Rye. It's a lovely market town and after a long day filming it's nice to get back to The Old Borough Arms, take Peggy for a walk and then call in for a drink at one of the town's excellent pubs. It's quite a tourist attraction and we even took the celebs there to run a Farmers Market in Series 2. Even the Lord Mayor and the Town Cryer turned up.

Rye is about 300 miles from my farm. It's great having Peggy with me. I love my dog and it's nice that I have a little bit of home with me while I'm away. Peggy and I always get up early and I take her to the beach for a long walk. There is a massive stretch of shingle beach on the way to the farm and we walk on there every morning and most nights too. She loves it especially when I throw a ball into the sea for her. It's a lovely way to start the day. She's also appeared in the show quite regularly.

Filming is harder than I thought. You are most conscious that you are working in a totally different environment to what is normal and the people around you are all TV stars or professionals in TV production. The days are long with 12 hours' filming each day being common. There is much waiting around as well.

Even though I feature a lot in the show there is a lot of down time when cameras have to relocate for different shots. When I know my next call time isn't for a while I take Peggy for another walk.

After the last day, we usually go back to film some promo shots which are used to open and close the show and also close-ups of me for my introduction. It takes quite a long time to get a few seconds of TV, but when it's put together it looks amazing!

It always fascinates me that after every day's filming, the material we have recorded is sent via email to London so they can start the edit.

Richard had told me he had a new team around him for Series 2 as he hadn't been happy with the way certain things happened the previous year. He explained the different ways things were going to work, knew exactly what he wanted and before I even got down to the farm I had a list of tasks and scripts emailed to prepare myself. I was emailed every day and now had my own FC script book. The transformation was incredible. We were no longer making it up as we went along, as it had been in Series 1.

Everything was much more organised, and we had a new producer, Dominic Pisani, a very professional, intelligent and fun young man.

When I arrived to start filming Series 2 the new series director Emmanuel Addo Jr came over to me and said, 'Are you FC? I've heard so much about you. It's a pleasure to meet you at last.' I was made up. He was great to work with and very organised, capturing some great shots of the cast.

I was way more confident this time. I had them weighed up. The celebs they'd gone for in Series 1 involved four very strong characters – Louie, Bobby, Charlotte and Megan – who all took over a bit.

One thing that really surprised me, particularly with the celebs in Series 2, was that they all loved being on the farm and close to the animals, maybe with the exception of Arge!

None of them had ever been so close to farm animals before and here we were asking them to go into the fields, gather sheep and then clip dirty wool off them, collect dung and many other tasks putting them completely out of their comfort zone!

In Series 2 we also had ewes lambing, which they all saw happen and some were in tears of joy.

As regular viewers will know, we award rosettes to the celeb that has performed the best on the day. We have a mock wooden field gate in the barn with all the celebs names on and we pin the rosettes on as they win them, just the way sheep farmers have them at an agricultural show.

They all become so incredibly competitive over the rosettes! Series 2 celeb David Potts likened them to having a Rolex!

The emotion within the barn when it gets to elimination time after day 3 is immense. No one wants to be first to go. In series 1 I didn't eliminate anyone on the first elimination day as they were all so good! This year was even worse, as to my mind they were all even better. We do build the drama of who's going and my goodness you can really feel the tension within the group – and behind the scenes too.

When I've made my decision about who goes that evening the only people who know are me, Stephen and two producers – and of course 'the channel' in that first year over 'WeWantAWomanGate!'

But, from that point, until we film it, everyone is trying to find out who's going! There are directors, camera operators, sound recordists, medics, security, runners, the farm staff and of course the celebs! Then we meet in the barn to do it. It is so tense. You can smell the fear!

We start off with the nice bits, talking about the day's events, who was good and what they had done. Then I award best in show. Then – the elimination. From a production point of view, I am asked before I say the name of the person to go, that I say, in true celeb reality show fashion, but with a rural twist: 'The person I am putting out to pasture tonight is ...'

I then look at each celeb for about 10 seconds so they can film it, then look towards the cameras in the gloom at the back of the barn where I can just about make out the producer who has his hand held high. When it drops, I say the name!

Farming, Celebs and Plum Pudding Pigs!

This is the worst bit because it seems to go on forever. It's also difficult to see because we have lights on us. My heart is beating hard at this point. But not as bad as the celebs! Then after the announcement the emotions start. Lots of tears and hugs between everyone. It's sad to see them go, but of course that's the nature of the show.

It's so nerve-racking when it's the last night too. But nicer, in one sense, as they've all reached the final. I have a group of people in front of me who are all hoping to win and of course only 1 can.

I remember Gleb Savchenko saying so many nice things after he won Series 1. Interviewed later by Stephen he came out with this: 'Have you had breakfast today?' he said. 'Then thank a farmer.' Nice.

They all go away enriched with the experience of farming, albeit in a showbiz sort of way. But it really puts a smile on my face to see these people, stars in their own right, brought right down to earth by this remarkable little show which hopefully not only brings entertainment to the public, but some knowledge about Britain's farmers and what we do to put food on their table every day.

First to leave the farm in 2019 was Tina Malone, a well-known and respected actress best known perhaps for her appearances in TV shows *Shameless* and *Brookside*. I'm afraid I didn't know of her, but she was a feisty little character and tried her very best. She was always cold and wore many layers of clothing every day! We had a very emotional moment together when I sat with her and bottle-fed baby lambs.

Next to be given his marching orders was Arg, or to give him his full name, James 'Arg' Argent from TV's *TOWIE*. Richard had told me that Arg was the most expensive celeb on the show, and since they get paid for the number of days that they last on the show in jest he intimated that I should feel free to get rid of him whenever

I liked. It wasn't a hard decision, probably my easiest of all to chuck him out.

Arg. Oh dear. He carries a bit too much weight, but it didn't stop him tackling the challenges. He did however have little energy or enthusiasm for farming and was very lucky to make week 2. He was always late in the morning and as Paul Merson said, he was a crap farmer! He is a very good looking young man and I'm sure he will do well. Just not on my farm! He didn't care about the tasks, didn't really like being there and wasn't really trying. The only reason he didn't go one day sooner was that Kadeena had to go to hospital, so we didn't send anyone home that day, but it was still going to be Arg.

To give him his due he knows how to play the social media and press game and is wonderful at promoting himself. He was never off his mobile phone and rang some of the paparazzi one day, who turned up while we were having lunch, using their ultra-long lenses from across the pond and road from where we were eating in the cartshed, to catch photographs of Arg eating salad, saying he was on a new fitness regime to do better at *Celebs on the Farm*!

Arg, together with David, did however contribute the most hilarious scene we've had in the first two series. Two big lads in a boat trying to clean out the pond. Everyone was in stitches – me, Stephen, the crew and all the celebs.

Kadeena (Cox) was my third eviction. This lady is a multi-gold-medal-winning Paralympian athlete. She won Gold at the Rio Olympics in 2016 in athletics and cycling. Wow! What a competitor! I didn't know of her, she suffers from MS and has faced so many challenges in her life. This hasn't stopped her getting to the top in her two sports and it certainly didn't stop her in this farm challenge. She wanted to win everything! Sadly, the pond challenge ended with Kadeena going to hospital as she was suffering badly. She missed a couple of challenges after this but did come back and tried her best. She didn't make the final but what a wonderful lady. A real honour for me to have met her. And she's from Yorkshire! Good lass!

It was to be a double-eviction the next time around and on this occasion it was to be world champion boxer Charlie and Queen of Benidorm, Crissy Rock.

Charlie (Edwards) came on the show as WBC Flyweight boxing champion, he retained his title twice during 2019, but is now going up in weight class to Super Flyweight. Wow again! That made two fabulous sports stars of the younger generation, he and Kadeena. What an honour it was to meet this extremely talented and enthusiastic young man.

He was so good at the tasks and bonded well with all the other celebs. He was so out of his comfort zone but tried his best at everything I gave him. It was a really tough decision to let him go and I really did miss him after he left. He even stayed an extra day after being eliminated because he didn't want to leave! A really special young man.

I love the TV show *Benidorm* and of course instantly recognised Crissy (Rock), who appeared in all of the first four series as well as appearing in others. She was a truly fantastic competitor and really embraced the farming life. She so wanted to win. We got on really well and the producers even made a funny clip of out-takes of the two of us supposedly falling for each other! Stephen even suggested there may be a farm marriage on the cards! Crissy was great but sadly didn't make the final. What a great lady though and I so enjoyed working with her. Crissy said, 'This is one of the best experiences I've ever had in my life!' She loved the close contact with the animals.

As I wrote earlier, for every day that a celeb is on the show it costs the show money. 'The channel' was going mad, because I wasn't getting rid of them and I ended up with five celebs getting into the final day. I had a massive problem with them all, because they were all good, as Crissy, Charlie and Kadeena had been too.

Hayley (Hughes) made it to the final five, but not to the last four as the final task before the final, shearing, was just a bit too much for this lovely girl. She just couldn't clip the sheep properly like the other four and she was absolutely mortified.

I do admit to having watched fleeting glimpses of Love Island, which is Hayley's claim to fame. I thought she would be first to go, because some might just categorise her, quite wrongly, the way people do of good looking, blonde girls. How wrong I was too. She had more determination than most and really tried her best.

Hayley really impressed me when the celebs were attempting to move sheep from one field to another. She knew exactly what to do. It was a shame some of the others didn't listen to her. The way she got stuck into everything, nothing fazed her. When she made the final day I was almost willing her to win, but she just failed on that one task and I sent her home. I loved her to bits, christened her my farmer's daughter for this series and was gutted when I had to say her time was up.

That left me with four celebs in the final, not three as we'd anticipated – David, Caprice, Artem and Paul. At least we had a lady in the final (Richard, I thought you'd like this little note) and by gum, what a lady!

My youngest son David used to have a poster of Caprice (Bourret) on his bedroom wall many years ago! She arrived on the farm a day later than everyone else due to business commitments and we had an altercation on day 1 when she questioned my judgement about her team's lack of success in the sheep herding challenge. I had her card marked and was ready to send her home early. I don't cope very well with hissy fits!

However, something just clicked in her and she was transformed. What a powerful, energetic woman. She wanted to win this and made the final. She proved to me that she had what it takes to perform well in the farming tasks and was so close to winning the title. One more day and I think she would have won it. She was so good to be around, and I really enjoyed her being one of the contestants.

I knew Artem (Chigvintsen) from watching TV's *Strictly* and he and Gleb, the Series 1 winner, are best mates. He had flown in from LA for the show and just like Gleb he was a very nice, personable young man and tried his best at all challenges. He was very consistent, interested in everything we did and was so close to winning. To come all that way to appear on our little show was quite special and he was a real pleasure to work with. Artem would have been an easy choice as a winner as he's a bit like Gleb, but I just felt he hadn't excelled.

When I first met David (Potts) I really wasn't sure what to think. Flamboyant, camp and very loud, I didn't expect him to stay for long. How wrong I was again, in a way, like with Hayley. David is the kindest, funniest and most enthusiastic young man with the most amazing laugh! I recorded his laugh as my phone ringtone! The scene with Arg in the pond was so funny and deserves a much wider audience. It's like something out of Laurel & Hardy.

He threw himself into every task, tight shorts and all, made the final and was within a whisker of winning. A truly lovely person. He first appeared on television as a club rep in the ITV show *Ibiza Weekender*. As an aside here I've always adored the *Ministry of Sound Ibiza Party Album*. If ever I'm home alone I blast out this fun party music as loud as I dare! Anyway, back to David. I'd never heard of *Ibiza Weekender* or him before, but he was an absolute pleasure to work with and such a friendly young man. He really took all the tasks very seriously.

And that left my winner of Series 2 as Paul (Merson). Now, of course I knew of Paul as I do follow sport. Paul wasn't just a footballer, he was an England international player, played in the World Cup Finals in 1998 and appears weekly on Sky Sports' *Soccer Special*.

Paul is a really friendly, down to earth person and we got along really well. He has had huge issues in his personal life which have affected him and by his own admission is scared stiff of animals. He was another I didn't expect staying too long, but he overcame his fears and worked hard at every task winning many of them.

When I first saw the look of terror on his face, going close to the animals, I saw in his eyes how petrified he really was. The one thing that really did it for me was the pig scene. Each of the celebs had to prepare a pig for showing, so that it looked the best it could be to go into the pig arena. I knew just how much this would take for him to overcome his natural fear. He was absolutely scared stiff and he'd been given a pig that was very temperamental. It was a recipe for disaster, but Paul did exactly the right thing. Before he started cleaning the pig he spoke to it, he calmed it. As he washed it, rubbed it and spruced it up he talked to it all of the time.

Paul made the most amazing transformation, overcoming all his fears and impressed me so much in all the tasks that I made him my Supreme *Celebs on the Farm* Champion 2019. A really special man and I am proud to have worked with him.

I think all of the celebs get a big shock when they come on the show. It's not an easy ride by any means. They think they may be going to a hotel every evening after filming, they don't! The only person who has done that in two series was Louie in Series 1, who said he just couldn't cope! Every other celeb has mucked in, as well as mucked out in many cases, and put up with living in their own motorhome on farmer Andrew's beautiful farm. There are no fancy facilities for them, although Natalie Woods is on hand to make sure they are looked after, particularly the girls, making sure the hair and makeup is right.

They all take part in real tasks around a real farm undertaking everything from shovelling shit to shearing sheep, ploughing a field to washing and feeding livestock. Then there are other more fun tasks like the partially naked calendar, raising funds for charity that we all posed for around the farm and selling sausages and soups on a market stall in Rye.

I enjoy every part of the show and being involved in the world of TV, and even when the celebs have all finished there is still work to do filming additional shots for the title sequence. I particularly loved the shots Richard, Dominic and Emmanuel came up with of my head moving from side to side, with the sounds they added that gave me this hard edge.

And that was it. Series 2 filming was done. The last of the celebs had gone to the cars they had waiting for them and were taken wherever they needed to be – at home, in Ibiza or wherever. For me it was time to take Peggy for a last walk, get us both in the car and head back north 300 miles to Spring View Farm in Thornton on the Hill in North Yorkshire.

CHAPTER 36

What's Next?

One thing I learned over the first two series of COTF – that's what we TV people call *Celebs on the Farm* in the trade – is that social media is a very powerful tool, specifically for self-promotion and since I'm now a part of this world and would love to do more TV work I've embraced it wholeheartedly.

After Series 1, I was still a social media virgin, but now I'm down with the kids – and everyone else – with thousands of followers on Facebook, Twitter and Instagram.

I realised that due to the success of the show there is now a Farmer Chris brand and we are building on it with a new website and this book with our wonderful publishers Great Northern Books and writer Chris Berry.

Chris is a multi-talented writer, author, singer-songwriter, TV presenter, singer-guitarist, entertainer and a great personal friend, who I approached to write this book for me.

It was Chris who first suggested we should launch this book on Open Farm Sunday, a national day designated for farms who wish to do so, to open their gates to visitors. We are certainly planning to be involved with Open Farm Sunday when coronavirus restrictions are eventually lifted and this is also where the future lies for Kate and I. We would love to launch Spring View Farm as an open farm for many events during the year. It may yet be Farmer Chris's Farm due to the branding!

We already have the Plum Pudding Pig Company

ready to sell meat from our Oxford Sandy & Black pigs; and visitors will be able to come and see our fantastic, beautiful Whitebred Shorthorn cattle. We'll have our neighbour Jacki Barlow with her alpacas, Nick Lupton will bring his portable hatchery so that people can see chicks hatching, the Rare Breeds Survival Trust with other rare breeds like Shetland sheep and plans are afoot for highly interactive days for families. Julian will also come to talk about his experiences as a vet and who knows, we might even try an action replay of our famous scene.

Crissy and Charlie have already said they would come along, which is really nice of them. I'd love to see all the celebs and the team at GooWoo come if they can. It's been one of the most exciting times of my life filming COTF and as this book goes to print I am filming a third series with Stephen for MTV this time. It's all very exciting.

We are not just filming a third series, we are also filming in my home county of Yorkshire at the beautiful Stepney Hill Farm near Scarborough, home of Ashley Tyson and his family.

I've been filming again this year with Julian for his latest series of *The Yorkshire Vet* and I've done a few other little TV jobs since Series 2 finished, but I've also found you have to be careful about what comes your way.

Some TV programmes have their own agenda and there was one programme where I felt it was a complete distortion of the facts in the way in which it had been edited. I've had invitations to go on GMTV to be interviewed by Piers Morgan, but it was about badger culling which is a very controversial subject and it would have been me against Brian May of the rock group Queen. I love Queen and their music, but I don't like what he is saying about us farmers. It just wouldn't work. I turned it down.

That's not the kind of TV work I enjoy. I don't want to be a pundit, someone drafted in to talk politics.

What I have found out about myself is I'm never satisfied. I always want something more. When I had my milk round I had to make it the biggest round Northern Dairies had in York. When I worked for Laycock's I had to beat its sales every year. When we bought Green's we had to get bigger and bigger. When we bought Sunnyvale, Wortley Cottage or Spring View Farm I wasn't happy until we'd totally renovated everything. I had to buy livestock straight away and went mad on buying. When I was younger I was never satisfied with the car I had.

My first wife Donna used to say, 'We live in hell. Only when we die will we leave hell and go to heaven.' A bit dramatic maybe, but I understand what she meant. Living in this world with all the associated issues and problems is very tough sometimes – and at times for me it feels like I'm under immense pressure to perform, to achieve in both my personal and business life.

My biggest regret in life was the failure of my marriage to Donna. It was mainly my fault of course, but I often reflect on how sad that was and that we produced two lovely boys who must have been terribly upset – and also that we missed out on being a true family because of the split and what pleasures that may have brought.

Whether subconsciously I am punishing myself for this big failure I don't know. All I do know is in relationships, business and material things Chris Jeffery never seems satisfied.

We already have plans well under way to change our lifestyle entirely by 2021 when Kate and I will both be 64 (I'm sure there's a song in there somewhere) and being able to farm in a different but special way. A way that helps rare breeds to survive, a way that embraces all that's good about British farming and being able to share that with the general public, perhaps including a holiday cottage, shepherds hut accommodation, farm shop and tearoom.

See what I mean, even then still never satisfied!

I've now appeared in three series of a TV show on Channel 5Star and MTV, but now I want to appear at the BAFTA awards for best reality show TV star! We were shortlisted in an awards last year! My book has to be a best-seller (no pressure Chris!). Is there any hope for me!!

It's actually quite remarkable that Kate and I still get on so well, but we do and we've been through an awful lot together. We have been to some amazing places all around the world and will hopefully get to many more but without doubt the best place of all is at home with my lovely Kate. She really, really is my rock and my life would be impossible without her. That's what I do know – and this bit ...

I enjoy being Farmer Chris.

EPILOGUE

I have learnt a huge amount about myself while writing this book. Especially about my mental health which has been challenged immensely over several periods of my colourful and turbulent life.

There is a white wooden sign in a roadside hedge as you approach Thirsk. It displays the next date of Thirsk Races and I used to get very excited seeing the date change regularly, as I loved going to the races.

At the end of the season in early September the sign is changed and it displays a date in April for the next meeting. The worst year of my life included feeling sick every time I passed this sign. It was April 15. The very date my trial was to start at Teesside Crown Court. It was almost like the sign had become a symbol of hatred for me and I struggled all year to remain stable.

TV presenter Caroline Flack recently took her own life and she was, like me, facing trial at Crown Court. I know there was some social media vitriol directed towards her, but my belief is she couldn't face the trial. I felt the same.

I remember Cliff Richard being treated in an appalling manner by the media and he too was to face trial. Thankfully he, like me, got a message from the CPS to say his case was being dropped as they had insufficient evidence to secure a conviction. This is not the same as being given an apology and told you are innocent. It still plays on my mind and I still have nightmares about it.

Kate and I have known four people in our circle of friends that have committed suicide in our area. Two male and two female. Both females were young, married and had young children. How distressing for them, as for all of us who knew them.

Each week farming sees at least one death by suicide, making it the highest rate of suicide in any industry in the UK. My mum tells me that my dad suffered from depression. I didn't know that. Even if I had, I wouldn't have known what to do to help.

You may think, by what you have just read in my book, that I have been a happy-go- lucky kind of guy who wears his heart on his sleeve and just gets on with life no matter what happens. Well, in the main that is true. But I realise that I do suffer with issues that I have never really talked about before.

I mean, come on, everyone has their fair share of problems, right? It's just how we deal with them. Some of us are better than others at this, but as we all know now, suicide is the cause of thousands of deaths in this country especially in men.

Back in 1995 when Donna and I had finally parted, I was in the most terrible state. Thankfully I received some counselling and I came through it. But I was close to ending it. Very close. In the worst year of my life when I was waiting to appear at court for an offence that I hadn't committed I was getting close again. I didn't, this time, travel to the train line, but I contemplated other ways.

I know this sounds awful but the pressure of running a business with an impending law case on top, as well as other pressures of life, almost broke me mentally. I know Kate suffered badly too. It was almost impossible to sleep. I turned to drink. I met with my GP and told him I needed help. He gave me some sleeping pills.

Recently, I applied for some life assurance cover with Aviva who I already have policies with. I was turned down. I couldn't believe it. I asked why and it transpires that my medical record shows that when I approached my

GP in the worst year of my life, that he recorded I was drinking a bottle of wine a day due to an impending court case. Aviva decided because of this I was now unfit to offer life cover. I was incensed about this as it was one incident that lasted a few months and for very good reason. I mean I had asked the GP for help and all he had given me was bloody sleeping pills!

Farming is the love of my life and it is hard. Bloody hard. Can you imagine how distressing it is to go into the field and find one of your cows licking its calf which is dead?

You can't be there all the time and this happens and we have to deal with it. You go and get a wheel barrow, put the calf in it, take it back to the buildings with a very distressed cow following and you're trying to explain to her what's happened! It's horrible.

We grow crops which can fail due to inclement weather conditions. This can result in thousands of pounds being lost. We, as farmers, try our best but sometimes it's just impossible. No wonder there is a high suicide rate. It's lonely too. Many farmers are on their own in remote parts of the country. Who do they talk to? They, like me, are maybe too proud to discuss their feelings.

Like I said at the beginning of this epilogue, I have learnt a huge amount about myself recently and that means I recognise for the first time in my life that mental health is a real issue for me and thousands of people like me. It really is time we all start to realise we must talk to each other more.

And cry! If you want a good cry, then do it! But do find help and talk to someone.

As I write this, my lovely country is in the grip of something never seen before. A hidden army which is attacking us from every which way. Covid19. We are all vulnerable and we are all scared. We don't know what's going to happen and we don't know when it's going to end. We do know that there will be more people than ever suffering with mental health issues and we must all recognise this and do more to help.

I will donate £1 from every book sold, via our shop and websites, to the National Suicide Prevention Alliance as I want to do my bit to try and help financially, but I hope that by reading this you too will be inspired to go out and do something too. If you know of anyone you suspect may be suffering from any mental health issue, give them a call or go and have a cup of tea with them.

It's nice to be nice you know.

ACKNOWLEDGEMENTS

My life story has had several twists and turns along the way and while on that journey I was fortunate enough to meet Chris Berry who I have known for over 20 years. He is a remarkable talent, being an author, journalist and accomplished musician and a true friend. Without his writing skills and patience this book would simply not have happened! So, my first thank you is to you Chris for the endless hours we spent together and for making this story into a comprehensible read. I really do appreciate what you have done for me.

Thanks also to David Burrill and his colleagues at Great Northern Books who have enough confidence in me to publish this book and also their great skills with the cover design and layout.

I must say a special thanks to Lou Cowmeadow (ex-Series Producer of *The Yorkshire Vet*) who recommended me to her friend Richard Woolfe for the role of Judge in *Celebs on the Farm*. Without her, this simply would not have happened. Also thanks to Richard Woolfe and business partner Paul Goodliffe (GooWoo Media) for taking me under their wing and having confidence in me to become their Judge on this wonderful, warm and funny TV show. A huge thanks also to all the crew at GooWoo who to a man/woman have all been very kind and supportive.

Stephen Bailey has become a great friend and colleague with his wonderful wit, charm and humour and I want to give special thanks to him for the help he has provided during filming and behind the scenes too. He is a very special person and I am sure he will become one of

Britain's top talents one day. "Love you babe!"

As my vet, Julian Norton was really skilful, carrying out some often-extreme operations on my farm, but also having a wonderful demeanour and sense of humour. We got on very well and the scene with Elsie my pig was one of the best ever on *The Yorkshire Vet*. I am convinced it was that which helped me achieve the interest of the producers in the TV world. Thank you Julian and I do wish you well in your new venture at Sandbeck Veterinary Practice in Wetherby.

Thanks to all the team at Green's Farm Supplies for covering the work while I am away filming! They have worked so well through the pandemic and deserve a special mention here.

All my friends and colleagues who have featured in the book deserve my thanks, as much of my life story revolves around them! Thank you all for your help, love and support over my several turbulent years. You have always been there for me and I really appreciate that.

My mum and dad have been the best parents I could ever have wished for. Sadly, Dad is no longer with us, but his memory lingers on and I love you both dearly. Thanks so much for everything.

Thanks also to my brothers Andy, David and Ian and their families for being a lovely family. We have never had a wrong word and your support is very special. My beautiful grandchildren William, Ryan, Marley, Maisie and Maddox, I love you dearly and I promise I will try to spend more time with you all.

I want to say a very special thanks to good friends Tim and Ann Robson for their friendship, but especially for their help when Kate had her accident. They dropped everything to help both me and Kate and I cannot thank them both enough.

Also, a big thank you to Richard and Janet Taylor who

are the kindest people I know and look after Kate so well when I'm away filming.

Finally, my lovely wife Kate. You are my best friend and my rock. I honestly do not know what I would do without you. What we have achieved together is incredible and you deserve a special award for putting up with me and my crazy ideas! Thank you so much. I love you dearly xx.

GREAT ORTHERN

www.gnbooks.co.uk